SPORTING
BODY
SPORTING
MIND

SPORTING BODY SPORTING MIND

An athlete's guide to mental training

JOHN SYER

CHRISTOPHER CONNOLLY

SPORTSPAGES

SIMON & SCHUSTER

A SPORTSPAGES BOOK
First published by Cambridge University Press 1984
Revised edition published by Simon & Schuster Limited 1987

Reprinted 1987

SPORTSPAGES
The Specialist Sports Bookshop
Cambridge Circus Shopping Centre
Charing Cross Road
London WC2H oJC

Simon & Schuster Limited
West Garden Place
Kendal Street
London W2 2AQ

Simon & Schuster of Australia Pty Limited, Sydney

British Library Cataloguing in Publication Data
Syer, John
  Sporting body, sporting mind : an athlete's
  guide to mental training.
  1. Sports — Psychological aspects
  2. Competition (Psychology)
  I. Title   II. Connolly, Christopher
  796'.01   GV706.4
  ISBN 0-671-65303-2

Printed and bound in Great Britain by
Anchor Brendon Limited, Tiptree, Essex

To George and Judith Brown, Moshe Feldenkrais, and Diana
Whitmore, who suggested new ways to view our experience.

Acknowledgements

The authors and publishers wish to thank the following for permission to reproduce
photographs.
  All Sport Photographic 39 (right), 143, front cover; Colorsport 7, 31, 138; Peter Dazeley 17;
Mick Eason 83; Lanny Johnson, Mountain Camera 90; Eileen Langsley (Supersport Photo-
graphic) 10, 18, 31, 89, (left), 46, 51; Nick Moody 147; Adrian Murrell 100; Sporting Pictures
(U.K. Ltd.) 110; Professional Sport 118; Bob Thomas 22, 57; Michael Zagaris 70.

Contents

Preface

by Sam Adams, Head Track and Field Coach, University of California at Santa Barbara.

In the world of sport today we are constantly concerned and confronted with problems and improvements in technical areas. We practise diligently to improve skills and develop muscular strength. We strive to improve physiological endurance, develop neuromuscular coordination and understand the principles of physics involved in athletic movements; we study strategy in team sports, utilise computers to determine tendencies and digitise ultra slow-motion films to study movement. We have also delved into the other area of the body-mind concept.

The psychology of sport is perhaps the real discipline that can make the difference between participation and being competitive. It is an area of development with which any athlete, in any sport, must be vitally concerned.

This guide by John Syer and Christopher Connolly is an excellent tool which the athlete can utilise personally to solve problems, prevent problems, and facilitate conceptual learning. It is a guide which should be studied by all coaches and trainers involved in any sport.

Most importantly, it is a guide which does not deal in generalities, but gives the athlete real tools with which to work. It has supreme practical value for those who wish to be totally prepared for the competitive athletic world of today.

Sam Adams

Preface

by Steve Perryman, Captain of Tottenham Hotspur Football Club 1975–85 and 1982 Footballer of the Year

I had never heard of mental training before John and Chris came to Tottenham. Gradually, I discovered they were presenting techniques which I now use instinctively but which had taken me a long playing career to discover. For me the key to success is to be prepared when I'm under pressure. I've seen John and Chris teach players how to achieve this in a very short time. They have a programme that's easy to understand and which is now here in book form.

I think the book will be of great interest not only to athletes but to coaches and managers too, particularly the sections on warming-up and team spirit. At Tottenham we used to spend so much time together without real communication. That changed when John and Chris came and I found I could captain the team better as a result. They have helped me get a clearer picture of the way that players think. For good or ill, thoughts and feelings affect our performance, although we rarely find time to discuss them. This book shows how to control and use them to our advantage.

The most common questions I'm asked are: 'Why can't Tottenham play well against bad teams, when they play so well against the best?', 'Why are we at our worst when we've just scored?' and 'Why don't we start playing until we're a goal down?' Anyone who thinks to ask such questions would find something interesting here.

My club has achieved many firsts. That our management had the foresight to introduce mental training gave me a real lift, for it showed that, despite our success, we were still striving to get further ahead. John and Chris became part of the team. They never seemed out of place, even in the team dressing room prior to a match. They gave us confidence both individually and as a group. This book explains how, and I recommend it to anyone wanting to improve their performance, whatever their sport.

Introduction

In March 1979, in London, we formed a consultancy called *The Sporting Bodymind*. Our idea was to encourage athletes and their coaches to explore the influence of thought and feelings on sports performance. Sportspeople ourselves of a certain athletic and coaching experience, we turned to our complementary experience of psychosynthesis, Gestalt, the Feldenkrais method and group dynamics and evolved a programme of practical exercises to present in the form of a weekend course. Before long we were working with individual athletes from a wide variety of sports and, in October 1980, we began a five-year association with Tottenham Hotspur Football Club. This book gives an account of our ideas and techniques and is illustrated by examples from our experience.

The book is addressed to 'you' the athlete but indirectly (and in the chapter on team spirit *directly*) to coaches as well. Indeed, although you can learn and practise most of the exercises alone, some require, and most would benefit from, the help of a coach. A few are best led by a sports psychologist but in most cases the technique of leading them can be learned without difficulty.

That said, we believe the sports psychologist would be a great asset to the coaching staff of any club or squad, so long as he is content to reflect and sometimes to guide the athlete's experience. Our own approach is firmly based in humanistic rather than clinical psychology and our prime concern is to *educate* rather than to cure ills or to carry out research. To this end we offer a *mental training programme* that can complement, enhance and perhaps streamline your physical training.

This does of course include helping you to seek out negative patterns of behaviour (the blocks to full expression of your potential) and to deal with the sort of problem encountered at one time or another by most athletes – anxiety, loss of concentration, inability to relax or to maintain form in the face of pressure and so on – but having been shown how to identify and deal with the problems, you can turn to techniques whose regular practice is bound to improve your sports performance.

In naming our consultancy we chose the word 'bodymind' to emphasise that while it is convenient to talk about body, mind and emotions, they operate as one unit. Hence, what you think affects how you feel and move, what you feel affects how you move and think, and how you use your body affects how you think and feel. *The Sporting Bodymind* and this book are designed to help you discover how *your* 'bodymind' determines your level of sporting performance.

We suggest you use the book as a practical manual. Each chapter presents a different aspect of mental training and supports the ideas, facts and theory with a programme of exercises. It is for you to put the exercises into practice, beginning with those that appeal to you most directly or speak to a particular need.

The appendices will enable you to use the book in a more methodical way. Appendix A presents a twelve-week course in basic *Sporting Bodymind* techniques. Appendix B is a checklist. Use this as you would the checklist of your car manual. When you are having some problem on the mental side of your performance, refer to the checklist and turn to the appropriate page for a suggested course of action. Appendix C gives an alphabetic listing of the techniques and exercises used in the book.

Despite the wealth of examples we have culled from working regularly with individual athletes in general and with Tottenham Hotspur Football Club in particular, the book is indeed addressed to the sportsperson at large. For this reason we have chosen to use a number of neutral words (such as 'sportsperson', 'athlete' and 'competition', rather than for example, 'player' or 'match') in order to make the book approachable to as wide a sporting public as possible. For the sake of simplicity we have used the pronouns 'he' and 'him' throughout, but the book is obviously intended for athletes of either sex.

One of our axioms is: 'If you know what you are doing, then you can do what you want.' A number of our techniques are designed to show how to recognise what you are doing and how your mind and emotions influence your performance. Once you have recognised these patterns, you can interrupt habits that you want to change and begin to introduce ones which are more productive. In this way you move towards realising your potential.

As an athlete, your potential is substantial, probably more than you allow yourself to imagine. The ability to realise that potential and perform accordingly is the mark of a champion. Increased self-knowledge, an enhanced sense of self-worth and the full expression of your ability follow one from another. We also believe that practising your sport may eventually lead to the realisation of your potential in all areas of life.

If you would like us to visit your club or Association, work with you on an individual basis, or are interested in the courses we run, please contact us at:

The Sporting Bodymind
18 Kemplay Road
London
NW3 1SY
U.K.
Tel: 01 435 8145

or: *The Sporting Bodymind*
P.O. Box 224
Birmingham
Michigan
48012
U.S.A.

1
WARMING UP

Most athletes recognise the need to warm-up. Even the most casual of Sunday morning footballers makes a show of jogging a few paces and touching his toes before looking around for the rest of his team. He knows, in theory at least, that stretching and warming his muscles makes him less prone to injury once the training or match begins.

However, warming-up is more than just a physical process. If you are to perform well you must also be mentally and emotionally prepared. You may begin your preparation some days before the event but what should you do once you have arrived at the place where the event is to be held? How can you best withdraw your attention from outside factors and focus it on (or *attune to*) those which will help your performance? This chapter gives a few suggestions.

Attunement

The verb 'to attune' means to 'become aware' or to 'focus attention'. The normal physical action of warming-up is that of 'attuning to' your body: focusing attention on its current state and attending to its needs, as a careful driver might check his engine before starting on a long journey. Through regular and careful 'attunement' you learn that these needs vary from day to day.

In fact, they also vary from individual to individual and if you are part of a team you probably arrive in time to do your own stretching before the team warm-up begins. When you are late and find yourself immediately involved in training or competition, you are not only more prone to injury but have difficulty in focusing your attention. This is because warming-up is not just a physical process. Instinctively, you use the time available for your physical warm-up to attune both to other aspects of yourself and to your surroundings.

The *mental* equivalent of the physical warm-up is that of concentrating on the task in hand; the *emotional* equivalent is 'psyching-up': getting

Peter Vidmar, U.S.A., warming-up prior to his bronze medal performance on the high bar, World Cup, 1982.

yourself in the right mood. In both cases, the process involves first noticing how far your thoughts and feelings are appropriate to the occasion and then finding a way of taking care of the distracting elements. Distractions that you don't recognise and deal with will invariably contribute to a below-par performance, however well-prepared your physical body might be.

How to attune

There are six different factors which affect our performance. In order to ensure an effective mental and emotional preparation – whether for a competition, a training session or a team meeting – it is best to consider each of these factors in turn. They are:

(i)   the place where you are to perform
(ii)   your body, thoughts and feelings
(iii) the individuals you are with
(iv)   the group or team of which you are a part
(v)   your objectives or purpose
(vi)   the activity or way in which you intend to reach those objectives

Attuning to the place

The environment of a competition can distract, be neutral or help the competitors. You have an advantage over your opponents if you are competing in a place where you have competed before and they have not. When you compete at home in front of sympathetic spectators you will probably benefit from their support. In some soccer Cup competitions, goals scored at home count for less than goals scored on an opposing team's ground, should the aggregate score over two legs be equal.

With time, the distracting peculiarities of a particular venue usually fade into the background but there are ways of speeding up this process. Identifying potential distractions in advance and becoming familiar or 'making friends' with them is a routine matter for many athletes and coaches. During one of the many interviews Virginia Wade gave after winning Wimbledon in 1977, she said she would go to Wimbledon in the morning and stand on court, imagining the match she was going to play there that afternoon, getting 'the feel' of the place. Lee Trevino, speaking of the difficulty European golfers can experience in America, says 'You must feel at home, any place you play.'

The concept of 'place' varies according to the sport. Indoor competitions are affected by floor surface, lighting, surrounding space, height of the ceiling, air currents and temperature. Outdoor conditions vary according to weather, ground conditions and setting. There are also other variables that are outside the structure of the competition which affect your concentration and should be considered. For instance, you may be affected by spectators and officials, and all venues have some intangible 'atmosphere' which might easily intrude upon your awareness.

If you are disturbed by hostile crowds or by poor decisions of the umpire or referee, your coach may simulate such circumstances in practice at home. With proper training, you can learn correct attitudes and reactions as readily as physical skills. The distraction must be simulated for two reasons: firstly, so that you may recognise the pattern of your reaction; and secondly, so that you may practise the technique to overcome the distraction.

There was a time when Russian teams were so unpopular in countries further West that their coaches would organise practice games at home with loudspeakers blaring the recorded sounds of a jeering crowd. The players became used to this before ever experiencing the real thing. Jupp Derwall, the West German soccer team manager, did a similar thing when he brought his team to Wembley in October 1982 to play England. Not only did he organise a training session for his young players on the Wembley pitch the day before the match but he asked for a recording of the 'Wembley roar' to be played over the public address system as his team came through the tunnel on to the pitch for that training.

When the Scottish volleyball team had a player who frequently lost his temper with the referee, thereby threatening the concentration of the whole team, the coach would ask the referees of certain practice games deliberately to penalise this player unfairly. Improving control over counter-productive emotions requires as much practice and attention as physical skills.

Once you have attuned to or 'made friends with' the environment of the competition, you sometimes have the chance to use it to your advantage. The Boston Red Sox baseball home ground at Fenway Park has a short left field wall. Therefore their batters practise hitting in that direction to get home runs. Queens Park Rangers take full advantage of the fact that they are the only team in the English football league to have a home ground with

Table 1 Dealing with a distracting environment

CHALLENGE	ACTION	
	Getting used to the place	*Making use of the place*
Physical distractions: Indoors: inappropriate lighting, floor surface, surrounding area, height of ceiling, air currents, temperature, etc. Outdoors: poor weather, ground conditions, setting etc.	Arrive early Identify supportive factors View the distractions in a larger context	Choose a position or an 'end' that is to your advantage In team sports, notice which team mates enjoy and can benefit from conditions that affect others adversely
Psychological distractions: Hostile spectators Inefficient officials	Simulate distractions in practice	Face the challenge collectively and turn it into a touchstone for team spirit Create and practise a positive response

artificial turf. Knowing that the ball comes off the ground fast when kicked over the defence, they can afford to play the off-side rule to its full advantage: if their backs make a misjudgement, it is still unlikely that an opposition striker would be fast enough to reach the ball.

Attuning to body, thoughts and feelings

Your thoughts and feelings probably vary more from day to day than do your physical sensations. A failed examination, an argument with a close friend, a complicated problem waiting to be solved may all drain much of your energy and attention from the task at hand. A golfer may spend his time at the office worrying about his putting and his time on the golf course worrying about his work. Often you may be present physically but for a moment still be mentally and emotionally held up somewhere else.

Unfortunately, you won't always realise that your attention is else-where. This means that you need to check each time, slowing down just enough for any underlying distractions to surface. The easiest way to do this is to sit down, let out a deep breath and *experience* yourself physically as being where you are. Then close your eyes and notice what's happening inside, especially any thoughts or feelings connected with what was happening to you before your arrival or is due to happen after you leave. The moment of physical quietness allows the background noise of thoughts and feelings to be heard and often to quieten down.

Unless the need for this kind of attunement is recognised by your coach, as a team athlete it will be more difficult to achieve because of the unvoiced pressure to interact with your team mates from the moment you arrive. Sometimes all you will be able to do is to make a point of telling someone else how you are feeling and anything pressing that concerns you. This will help you to identify your personal concerns and put them to one side.

This process may be reinforced by an exercise that is particularly effective if you can find somewhere to be on your own. It allows the part of yourself that wants to participate in the training session or the competition to make a promise to the part which has other needs that these will be met later on when you can deal with them properly.

Initially, the exercise is best led by your coach, or by a fellow athlete.

- Sit quietly, close your eyes, take a deep breath and allow yourself to settle heavily into your chair as you breathe out slowly.

  Imagine yourself sitting at a desk in front of a window. Look out and notice what you see, what the weather is like, what movement there may be. Then look down at the desk and notice a blank sheet of paper and a pen. Pick up the pen and write down whatever is worrying or exciting you, anything you identify as a distraction. As you write, see the shape of your handwriting on the page, hear the point of your pen slide over the paper, feel the weight of your upper body on your arm. If you find it easier, you can draw a picture to represent the distractions or your distracted mood. When you have finished put down the pen, fold up the piece of paper and turn around. You see a box behind you. It may be on a shelf or on the floor. Notice how large it is, what colour it is, whether it is in the light or the shadow. Open the lid. Then put the folded piece of paper inside the box, close the lid and turn back to the desk, settling back into your chair and once more looking out of the window.

Having done this, you can open your eyes, ready to interact with those around you. However, it is important that once your session or match is over, you again close your eyes and go back to this imaginary desk, turn around, open the box, get out and unfold the piece of paper and look to see what you wrote or drew. Sometimes this will no longer be of interest and that's fine but, if the exercise is to continue to work – and with time it can become increasingly effective – the part of you that has been promised attention later on must learn to trust that it will get that attention.

We first developed this technique with Barbara Lynch, who subsequently won the 1979 European 15 Trench Trap-Shooting title. There are innumerable distractions that can occur between shooting and preparing for the next shot – other shooters can kick empty cartridges or eject their spent shells in your direction, or a trap machine may break down just as you begin to shoot. Barbara found she was able to pull her attention back to her shooting by finding an image for the distractions and putting that image into a black box behind her. Much later, a Scottish gymnast found this exercise so effective that she was once able to ignore blisters on her hands by 'putting them in her black box'.

Attuning to people and equipment

Your performance is also affected by your relationship to your opponents and to members of your own team. (We look again at reactions to opponents in chapter 7.) When warming-up, you should tune in to people on your own side – whether to members of your basketball team, to your track coach, or to your caddy – after tuning in to yourself.

You can do this through conversation and shared action. Talking to individuals on your own side before the event begins can open the way to increased awareness of those individuals during play. Detailed discussion of aims and tactics is only marginally more useful than conversation about matters unrelated to the coming competition.

What counts is the element of concern, a sense of putting aside differences for the duration of the competition and an appreciation of the other person's strength. If this is a competition warm-up, the time for criticism is past. Should you have something critical to say it is better to wait until you are meeting to prepare the next event.

A coach with a team or squad does well to give new athletes, athletes who have been away and those who are in any way agitated the chance to speak before he takes over. With some team sports, discussion, appreciation and encouragement can be complemented by skills practice in pairs, taking the individual physical warm-up one step nearer to the actual competition format. Volleyball teams usually warm up in pairs on court before the spiking practice begins and, in doing so, all players tune in closely to one other player. It is often better for the coach to designate the pairings with a view to reinforcing those personal connections within the team which are most important. In East Germany, senior members of a volleyball team will be given a young player to work with and encourage, over a long period of time.

It is at this stage of your warming-up that you should tune in to your equipment or, if you are a jockey or a show jumper, to your horse. Hearing a sailor we worked with suddenly say 'I love sitting in my boat!' and learning how much care and attention he'd lavished on his rudder that particular week, was to recognise the same depth of feeling as an American horsewoman had expressed for her horse. Both of those athletes were also, in some important sense, part of a team. Before their competitions, they each tuned in to the positive feelings they had, one for his boat, the other for her horse, in much the same way that the two of us might attune before a *Sporting Bodymind* course or that Bob Hewitt might attune to Frew McMillan.

Attuning to the team

If you are part of a team you should now attune to team spirit and attend to your needs as a group. Only a team that is well attuned draws the most from the strengths of its individual members.

Nor is it only team sport athletes who need to attune to team spirit. Once the golfer and his caddy have acknowledged each other, they tune into their strength as a unit. Many individual athletes feel part of such a unit and able to tune into a similar 'energy field'. Daley Thompson, the British decathlete, an individualist within a squad, has nevertheless spoken of the lift he gets from his 'team' of helpers, friends and family. Yannick Noah, after winning the 1983 French tennis championships, said 'I am doubly happy because I didn't win this alone. It was with my family, my friends and the French Federation. It's *our* victory.'

Athletes, swimmers and riders can all contribute and draw upon team spirit. For them, the sense of being part of a team is particularly strong when, although points are given for each individual success, the winner is the squad with the greatest number of points at the end of the event.

We suggest ways of generating and fostering team spirit in chapter 8. Calling on that team spirit is one of the final stages of warming-up. It may be some ritual movement or vocal expression or it may be a coach giving his final pep-talk but it is always designed to evoke a shared mood of strength and confidence.

The gradual rise in emotional temperature in the Tottenham dressing room, prior to a match, was an exhilarating experience. Early on, Ray Clemence asked the time every ten minutes (as much to ensure that others were aware of it, as to inform himself), but as the quiet checking out process in pairs gave way to banter and more generalised shouts, Peter Shreeve, the

Seve Ballesteros and caddie Peter Coleman – working together as a unit.

coach, would chime in with 'Six minutes to go!' and even the youngest substitute could be heard shouting 'Come on then, lads!'

The ritual concluded with every player moving around the central table and tapping every other player on the back: 'All the best, Chris!', 'All the best, Glenn!', 'All the best, Graham!'—until they ended in a bunched-up line behind Steve Perryman who, turning back with a last 'Come on the boys!' opened the dressing-room door.

Attuning to purpose

Team spirit turns your attention and energy away from yourself and towards a common objective. This objective must be realistic, challenging and agreed. Long-term objectives will have been decided at the beginning of the season and then periodically reviewed and brought up-to-date.

As an individual athlete, whether really alone or part of a team, you should have set yourself personal goals at the beginning of the week that are steps on the way towards perfecting your own performance. If you are part of a team, these goals will be related to the team's objective, which in turn will have been decided at an earlier team meeting. *Immediately before the competition*, this purpose should be reaffirmed, either by you to a friend or, if you belong to a team, by your coach in his pre-match pep-talk. This should be done simply and without lapsing into discussion. Your purpose is long decided and is repeated now as a kind of rallying call.

U.S.A. Women's Lacrosse team – 'psyching-up' prior to match.

Attuning to the activity

Once you have reaffirmed your goals, you should quickly review *the way* in which you are going to achieve them – the drills you want to perform in a training session or your tactics for a competition.

If you are about to compete, either your coach will remind you of the

Table 2   Warming-up

STAGE	ASPECT	OBJECTIVE	EXERCISE
1	Place	(i) Get used to external distractions (ii) Make use of external distractions	Build distractions into practices during training Arrive early Discuss distractions with team mates
2	Body, thoughts and feelings	(i) Ease physical ills, prevent injuries and arouse physically (ii) Deal with distracting thoughts and feelings	Massage Individual stretching and skill work Individual pep-talk or relaxation *Black box* visualisation
3	Other people and equipment	(i) Put aside disagreements (ii) Tune into strength and confidence of two-person team spirit (iii) Reinforce intuitive anticipation	East European pairs system Talking to one another Skill practice in pairs Pay attention to equipment
4	Team	(i) Tune in and heighten team spirit, strength, energy and intuition	Small group discussions Small group skill practice Full team pep-talk
5	Purpose	(i) Channel the aroused spirit etc. towards specific agreed goal	Set goals at prior discussion meetings. Full team pep-talk based on those meetings
6	Activity	(i) Reaffirm the *way* of achieving the goal (ii) Take away pressure to win and increase incentive to improve	Decide tactics at prior discussion meetings Give brief reminder of tactics Prepare analysis sheets

tactics you decided earlier in the week or you will rehearse them mentally yourself. Prior to a competition, focusing on *how* you will achieve your goals rather than on the goals themselves will allow you to channel all your energy towards some specific action that you feel confident of being able to perform.

Warming-up is a personal process and it is for you to discover by trial and error what suits you best. Normally it will include attuning to factors that would otherwise affect your performance adversely. Some of these, such as faulty equipment or too much physical tension, you will be able to change. Others, such as the weather or your opponents, you will be unable to control and these you must deal with by changing *your response* to them.

There are also factors which will be supportive to your performance. These too you will discover as you first turn your attention outwards to your environment, then inwards to your body, thoughts and feelings and then outwards again to your team mates, your goal and your tactics. In the end you will have acquired an exhilarating sense of being prepared and responsible for your own performance.

2
BODY AWARENESS

Why include a section on the body in a book about mental training?

Our main focus here is not physical training but the relationship of body to mind. However, in this specific sense, body *awareness* is important since it is a first step towards relaxation, visualisation and changing ineffectual patterns of movement.

Ultimately it is the quality of the body-mind relationship – its cultivation or neglect, the degree to which you maintain harmony and co-operation – that determines how far you tap your full potential as an athlete.

In this chapter we explore the nature of this body-mind relationship and detail exercises which will set you on the way to developing an accurate awareness of your body.

Communication

Athletes who ignore the delicate balance of a healthy body-mind relationship bring untold hardship on themselves. All too often one aspect is exaggerated at the expense of another. The assertion that 'The best thing I can do is ignore my thoughts completely. The mind is just a troublemaker,' is almost as common as its converse 'If I put my mind to it, I can make my body do whatever I want. It's just a question of will power and shutting off the pain.' In practice, neither works. When you try to ignore your mind, it finds its own ways of intruding, distorting, misbehaving or otherwise making its presence known. On the other hand, serious physical injury, intense mental stress and a lopsided personality which functions poorly outside the sporting situation can all result from a rigid application of the 'mind over matter' theory.

The correct approach lies somewhere between these two extremes. Most of this book is designed to develop a language which can improve communication between mind and body. In a number of chapters we give precise suggestions for using the mind to guide and direct the body and emotions. However, it is just as important that we establish the habit of listening to the demands of the body. Effective communication is a two-way

Overleaf: Judy Livermore, England – perfect body-mind relationship.

process: if you are to communicate properly with your body, you must understand what your body is saying to you. It is not enough to berate it with worn-out demands such as :'Move!', 'Faster!', '*Hold* it! What's wrong with you? Steady!', etc. To educate your body, you must know how it functions and learn its language.

Education

Once an effective communication system has been constructed, educating your physical self involves four key processes. These are learning, training, maintenance and change.

Learning

From the day we are born we continually learn how to improve our physical performance. Unlike the new-born calf that can stand a few hours after birth, it takes a baby nine to twelve months to learn to stand and walk, and then several years to learn to throw or kick a ball with any degree of control. The way we sit, walk, talk, brush our teeth and tie our shoe laces are all learned. In fact, any activity which we pursue with dedication and purpose involves learning to use our body and manipulate our environment. Sports training is focused on the process of acquiring skill and becoming consistent in its performance. Mental training is often concerned with the process of *learning to learn.* The easier, quicker and more efficiently we are able to learn, the easier, more effective and better we will be able to perform our sport.

Because we have to learn so much of our behaviour rather than its being 'programmed' through instinct or wired into our nervous system, we have a tremendous ability as a species to perform *old* activities in *new* ways and even to do new things never before considered possible, perhaps never before imagined. Almost all of sport, with the exception of running, jumping and perhaps climbing, involves using our bodies in ways which are not necessarily implicit and certainly not predetermined in our central nervous system. Many of our sports have been slowly cultivated over the centuries. Military sports such as archery and throwing the javelin go back thousands of years, other sports such as golf and lacrosse have been played for hundreds of years, whilst some, such as windsurfing and hang-gliding, are still in their infancy. The physical skill required for these sports is created through the ingenuity of our psyche and the plasticity of our nervous system. High jumper Dick Fosbury, in creating the Fosbury Flop, gave a classic example of finding a completely new solution to an old challenge.

The great disadvantage of our open-ended learning ability lies in the fact that we can learn to do things in the 'wrong way'. Any coach taking on a group of youngsters who have been trained poorly has to contend with this. A great part of physical training involves beginning to recognise and isolate bad habits in order to interrupt them.

Only then can you introduce more appropriate methods of using your body and achieving your objective. Cultivating good habits and eliminating bad ones is the way that we learn and the main objective of all sports training.

Training

Physical training has two main benefits. On the one hand you train to improve your physique. Resistance training increases the strength and tonus of the various muscles and organs. (Specific exercises increase the strength of those muscle groups most used in the practice of your particular sport.) Endurance training increases the stamina of your heart and lungs. Training also establishes the proper ratio between fat and muscle and includes balancing the intake of carbohydrates, fats, proteins, vitamins and minerals through proper diet.

On the other hand, you also train in order to increase your ability to perform various skills: your backhand in tennis, dribbling in basketball, hand to eye co-ordination in shooting, stable positioning of the body in archery and so forth. When you practise these skills you are training more than muscles. Repetition of physical skills sends a constant stream of signals via your nervous system to the brain, familiarising it with the movement. What repetition really does is to *train the nervous system and the brain.*

An incredibly sophisticated and yet remarkably simple relationship exists between your nervous system and your body. When you move, your body sends thousands of signals every second to the brain which, in turn, collects, organises and distils them into some cohesive whole. The brain then makes decisions (some conscious, most unconscious) and sends signals back through your nervous system which breaks them down into simpler and more precise messages for each muscle fibre, gland and organ. It is as if the two halves of a conversation are happening at once, information being constantly given and received through the medium of your nervous system.

Training allows you to 'package' the information appropriately so that nervous system and body can take over. Several million years of evolution combined with your learning experience know best how to organise the minutiae of movement. Imagine trying consciously to co-ordinate the various muscle groups required to perform a vault in gymnastics or negotiate your way down a slalom course on skis. Better to let your body get on with it!

Maintenance and change

Nonetheless if you are to improve your physical performance you must first discriminate between that part of your technique you want to keep and the part you want to lose. Consciously controlling this process of maintenance and change is easier said than done.

Man is indeed a creature of habits. When we learn, we are constantly encountering habitual patterns of movement and thought. When we train we are attempting to keep the habits which work and change the ones which don't. If I have settled into a good golf stroke, the last thing I want to do is tinker with it. I want to *maintain* it. I do this by giving it regular, but not too close, attention. I re-energise it regularly through practice but try to keep my awareness of it at a constant level, giving it neither too much nor too little attention.

But if my putting is on the rocks (and whose putting has never been on the rocks!) the amount of energy and attention I put into it can in some cases be limited only by the hours of daylight available. I *change*, tinker and adapt, until finally some new stroke settles into place and begins to work for me. Then I again shift back to my maintenance pattern and do what is necessary to hold it without meddling. This constant shuttling back and forth along the continuum of maintenance and change constitutes the fundamental process of training and takes place through the whole range of skills and techniques. The flow chart shows how this process works when learning a stroke in squash.

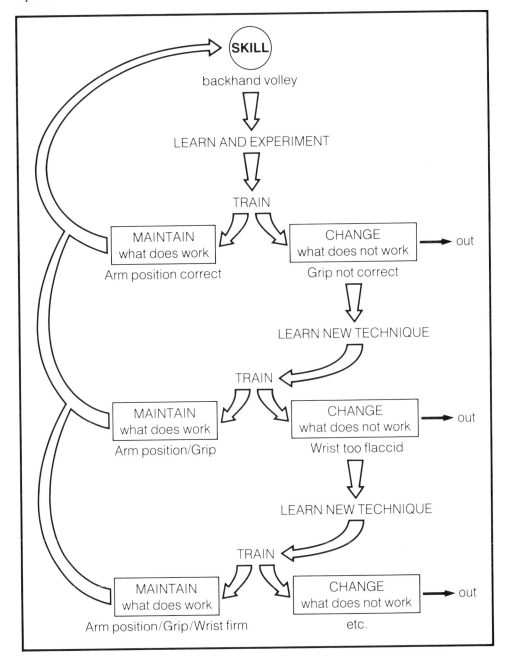

Body awareness exercises

The following exercises are designed to accomplish two things. Firstly, they will help you become more aware of what you are doing as you perform your sport, thereby giving you greater freedom to choose what to maintain and what to change. Secondly, they will give you some insight into your body-mind relationship by presenting habitual activities or experiences in a new context. One of the best ways of increasing body awareness is to do habitual things in non-habitual ways. If you try to maintain awareness whilst practising habitual activities in habitual ways, you will probably soon find yourself thinking about something else.

1 *Kinaesthetic body inventory*

The kinaesthetic sense is an expansion of the sense of touch. It includes the feeling of rough and smooth, soft and hard, hot and cold, wet and dry, but it particularly includes the signals and information which allow you to recognise and remember your own movement. It is the *internal* information which your body is constantly giving itself about balance, movement and the relationship of parts of the body to each other: information about what it feels like to function. Obviously, the role that this sense plays in moving and learning is central.

One of the main problems in learning any skill is to be really aware of what your body is doing, particularly in the parts *other* than those you normally attend to. This exercise will help you to extend your awareness throughout your body. It can be practised at any time. (It can also be used to deepen relaxation, as we shall see in the next chapter.) If you are in a sitting position, start the exercise from the head downwards, if lying down, follow the feet to head routine we describe opposite.

Once you have done this exercise by itself, you can take it a step further. When you are doing any training which is repetitive, go through this body inventory whilst you actually practise. When running, start at your feet and slowly move through your body, noticing how each part functions as a part of the whole. As you practise your ground strokes in tennis, put your attention into different parts of your body. Whilst you swim, go through this inventory. You will find it to be a remarkably useful experience and one that substantially enhances your efficiency of movement.

2 *Eyes closed practice*

This exercise is an effective way of improving the level of performance of certain closed skills (for example, free throw shots in basketball, tennis serves, bowling in cricket). Find a time and place where you can practise a particular closed skill with your eyes closed without danger or embarrassment. First, practise it with your eyes open as you would normally – for example, bowling a series of balls. Then stop.

Now close your eyes and, in the same place, perform the same skill several times with your eyes closed. Become aware of how you feel. What do you hear? How do you orient yourself? How do you use your

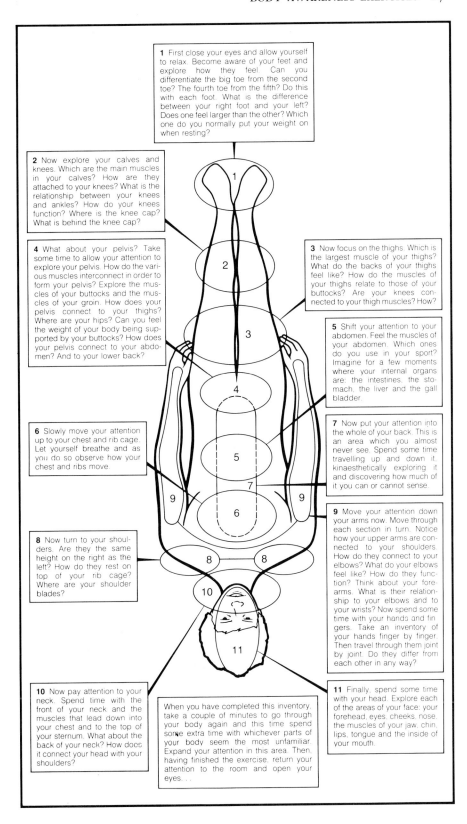

1 First close your eyes and allow yourself to relax. Become aware of your feet and explore how they feel. Can you differentiate the big toe from the second toe? The fourth toe from the fifth? Do this with each foot. What is the difference between your right foot and your left? Does one feel larger than the other? Which one do you normally put your weight on when resting?

2 Now explore your calves and knees. Which are the main muscles in your calves? How are they attached to your knees? What is the relationship between your knees and ankles? How do your knees function? Where is the knee cap? What is behind the knee cap?

4 What about your pelvis? Take some time to allow your attention to explore your pelvis. How do the various muscles interconnect in order to form your pelvis? Explore the muscles of your buttocks and the muscles of your groin. How does your pelvis connect to your thighs? Where are your hips? Can you feel the weight of your body being supported by your buttocks? How does your pelvis connect to your abdomen? And to your lower back?

3 Now focus on the thighs. Which is the largest muscle of your thighs? What do the backs of your thighs feel like? How do the muscles of your thighs relate to those of your buttocks? Are your knees connected to your thigh muscles? How?

5 Shift your attention to your abdomen. Feel the muscles of your abdomen. Which ones do you use in your sport? Imagine for a few moments where your internal organs are: the intestines, the stomach, the liver and the gall bladder.

6 Slowly move your attention up to your chest and rib cage. Let yourself breathe and as you do so observe how your chest and ribs move.

7 Now put your attention into the whole of your back. This is an area which you almost never see. Spend some time travelling up and down it, kinaesthetically exploring it and discovering how much of it you can or cannot sense.

8 Now turn to your shoulders. Are they the same height on the right as the left? How do they rest on top of your rib cage? Where are your shoulder blades?

9 Move your attention down your arms now. Move through each section in turn. Notice how your upper arms are connected to your shoulders. How do they connect to your elbows? What do your elbows feel like? How do they function? Think about your forearms. What is their relationship to your elbows and to your wrists? Now spend some time with your hands and fingers. Take an inventory of your hands finger by finger. Then travel through them joint by joint. Do they differ from each other in any way?

10 Now pay attention to your neck. Spend time with the front of your neck and the muscles that lead down into your chest and to the top of your sternum. What about the back of your neck? How does it connect your head with your shoulders?

When you have completed this inventory, take a couple of minutes to go through your body again and this time spend some extra time with whichever parts of your body seem the most unfamiliar. Expand your attention in this area. Then, having finished the exercise, return your attention to the room and open your eyes...

11 Finally, spend some time with your head. Explore each of the areas of your face: your forehead, eyes, cheeks, nose, the muscles of your jaw, chin, lips, tongue and the inside of your mouth.

non-visual senses to organise your movement? Pay particular attention to your kinaesthetic sense.

Then open your eyes and go back to practising in the normal way. After a time, stop and practise again with your eyes closed. As before, concentrate on your movement and what it feels like to perform the activity with your eyes closed. Open them periodically to check on the results. Do you find that what you thought you were doing is actually what is happening when you open your eyes? What is different and how can you adjust the discrepancies kinaesthetically rather than visually?

Now practise again with your eyes open and then shift from eyes-open to eyes-closed practice several times, experiencing the sense of moving and getting the right results. What do you do with your body and kinaesthetic sense in order to practise as efficiently as possible? Then finish the exercise with a final eyes-open practice.

3 *Colour coding body*

This is another simple exercise which increases body awareness and can also add an extra dimension to the mental rehearsal techniques described in chapter 4. Close your eyes, relax, and, in your imagination, set the scene for a particular action or skill that you want to practise. Now watch yourself practising the skill. Make certain that as you create these pictures of yourself moving, you are watching yourself as if from the outside.

Then imagine that you see each area of your body surrounded by a colour. You can see your head, arms, neck and shoulders moving as if behind or enveloped in the colour blue. Still performing the same skill, notice that your torso, waist, pelvis and hips seem to be surrounded by the colour green . . . and as you shift your attention to your legs, you see that your thighs, knees, calves, ankles and feet are surrounded by the colour red.

From time to time, use this colour coding system as you mentally rehearse a skill. It is an excellent way of helping you isolate different parts of your body, when you want to pinpoint the influence that a particular part has on the overall performance of the skill you are rehearsing.

If you find this exercise valuable, and are fairly good at visualising, you can expand the system to include all the colours of the rainbow. Your feet and ankles might be red, your calves, knees and thighs orange, your pelvis yellow, your torso green, your shoulders sky-blue, your arms indigo, and your head and neck violet.

4 *Breathing*

In our chapter on relaxation and concentration we describe breathing as a prime technique in increasing control over the functioning of your body. Here is a preliminary breathing exercise which helps increase body awareness.

Begin by choosing a skill you want to improve and practise this skill physically. As you repeat the skill, begin to take note of your breathing pattern. Is there a relationship between your breathing and the movement sequence? When do you inhale? When do you exhale? When do you hold your breath? Continue your physical practice whilst keeping track of how you breathe.

After a while, introduce some change into your breathing pattern. Inhale when you normally exhale. Exhale when you normally inhale. Breathe when you would hold your breath. Breathe faster or slower than your normal speed. In other words, vary your breathing pattern so that you begin to notice how your breathing influences your performance.

After you have varied your breathing for a while, stop. Return to your original pattern. Notice the difference in your breathing. How do you use your body now? In particular, be aware of your ribs and chest and how these parts of your body now participate in the breathing movement.

5 *Changing handedness*

If you are a right-handed player and playing a game which requires specialisation of one side of your body (for example, tennis, baseball, cricket, squash), try practising with the other hand. Some of baseball's most famous batters have been 'switch hitters' and many top level strikers in soccer are two-footed. Why not you?

However, the prime purpose of this exercise is to notice how you approach the skill, and particularly what you do with the rest of your body to organise it around the new use of the opposite side. It gives you an opportunity to gain insight into problems which are otherwise masked by the overall competency of your technique. Some of the small but important details are not readily noticeable with your normal handedness but rapidly become prominent on the opposite side.

6 *Exaggeration*

Another way of learning about your body is to exaggerate movements. Not surprisingly, exaggeration highlights those parts of your movement which are under control and those which are not. By exaggerating a golf swing, for example, you gain awareness of the finesse you were looking for.

Exaggerating a mistake can also be an enlightening technique. When you find yourself making a mistake repeatedly, try exaggerating it. Let the mistake override all other aspects of your skill so that you fully experience what you are doing. This serves two purposes. It means you acquire a complete and measurable experience of what you are doing and how the mistake influences the rest of your body. It also allows you to release some of the frustration which will have been making you tense. The tension itself will have kept you from performing the movement as you wished. Remove the frustration by exaggerating the mistakes, take a moment to calm down and then imagine yourself performing the movement correctly. When you have done this and are ready to practise again, do so, allowing yourself to embody what you visualised.

- *7 Key movements*

Most of us at an early age become accustomed to the shouts of 'Keep your eye on the ball!', 'Follow through!', 'Keep your head down!', 'Keep your weight forward!' and other similar instructions. They are usually made with good reason, highlighting key elements of technique which, when incorporated into your play, enhance your performance.

However, as we shall explain in chapter 5, such instructions tend to inhibit rather than promote the desired effect and once your coach has analysed the change that you need to make, it is better that he leads you to this change through an awareness of what *is*. This approach asks that you focus attention on the key movement with interest and turn your judgemental ability to making a finely accurate assessment of what you are doing, rather than of what you may believe you should be doing. Sooner or later a smoother, more relaxed and more enjoyable performance of the action will begin to happen, as if of its own accord.

Psychophysical re-education

As sports training becomes ever more sophisticated and biomechanics and kinesiology lead coaches and physiotherapists into ever finer analyses of movement, it has become clear to us that there is a need for a reorganisation of movement education towards the whole human being and away from its obsession with strict performance functioning goals.

Of all the systems of movement education which we have explored, the one called the 'Feldenkrais Method' stands out as being the most beneficial for athletes. Dr Moshe Feldenkrais, an Israeli scientist (physicist by training and founder of the French Judo Club), has developed a subtle and sophisticated system for educating the body to move with minimal effort in order to produce maximum results. The system helps you increase awareness of your movement and of the learning process whereby you create change in its organisation. The key to optimum performance and learning lies in your conscious ability to recognise inefficient movement, interrupt the habitual pattern and reorganise the movement into an appropriate pattern. Feldenkrais has applied his system not only to athletes and members of the Israeli Olympic team, but to dancers, stroke patients, individuals recovering from injuries and people suffering from neuromuscular disorders such as cerebral palsy and muscular dystrophy.

The value of the method for sportspeople lies in its ability to teach the body to learn to function as a whole. Individual movements are differentiated and then reintegrated on a higher level of organisation. The system is not a physical fitness system. It educates the nervous system to discriminate

Top: A 'Fosbury Flop' jump from Sara Simeoni, Italy's former world record holder. This demonstrates a classic example of finding a completely new solution to an old challenge.

Bottom: Olga Corbutt from the U.S.S.R. – complete equilibrium achieved through years of intense training.

between the different qualities of movement and to take this information into the sporting situation.

Since the object of this book is ultimately to help you expand the control over your physical performance, any system which improves your ability to learn in this way enhances your overall performance. The systematic differentiation of the ways in which the body moves and learns to function can be taught and enhanced considerably through the practice of these psychophysical re-education exercises. Each sport requires a specialised series of lessons in movement differentiation which are specific to the range of skills that make up the complete performance. Further information on these exercises can be found in *Awareness Through Movement* (Harper and Row, 1972) by M. Feldenkrais.

3
RELAXATION AND CONCENTRATION

These two related skills are important both for individual and team athletes. Relaxation is a temporary and deliberate withdrawal from activity which, if correctly timed, allows you to recharge and make full use of your physical, mental and emotional energy. Concentration is a withdrawal of attention from factors which are no longer or have never been relevant to your immediate performance to focus it on those which are.

Here we discuss why, when and how to relax and concentrate, suggesting some exercises which will help you develop these skills.

Relaxation

What is relaxation?

Physically, emotionally and mentally, relaxation is characterised by an absence of activity and tension: it is a period of stillness when you've let go of all sense of need. Degrees of relaxation and tension exist on a continuum. With practice you can discover which point on that continuum is right for you at any particular time. Learning to relax is an ongoing process, but for the time being you should consider the most relaxed state that you experience as your personal base or 'zero arousal level'. Zero arousal, arousal and over-arousal are points on this same continuum, although varying in terms of measurable relaxation or tension from athlete to athlete.

You are probably relaxed, if not always completely so, when you're asleep, but when you use relaxation to benefit your sports performance, you should make sure that you remain alert to impressions that come from within or from outside yourself.

Your levels of physical, emotional and mental relaxation may vary at any given time but they are closely related and arousal on one level is likely to provoke arousal on another. At the same time, it is possible to lower the level of arousal on any one of the three levels by increasing the degree of relaxation on another. Smiles and laughter or soothing music will tend to ease mental stress, slower, deeper breathing will lessen anxiety or anger, and a period of

Overleaf: Alex Higgins – intense concentration.

quietly watching your thoughts go by will allow excess tension to drain from your body.

Why relax?

The degree of relaxation appropriate for an athlete will vary from individual to individual and from occasion to occasion.

■   learn to relax and withdraw *completely*
(i) to acquire a point of reference, a recognition of your own 'zero arousal level'
(ii) to increase awareness of your own physical, mental and emotional resources and how best to use them
(iii) to learn to recognise your patterns of behaviour and thence to begin to change those that inhibit your performance
(iv) to gain a detached impression of your environment
(v) simply to experience a positive, pleasurable and beneficial state of being that allows regeneration of body, mind and emotions – complete relaxation can enable you, when under prolonged and excessive pressure, to rediscover pleasure in your sport

■   learn to relax *momentarily*
(i) to reduce *over*-arousal to a manageable and productive level, during and immediately prior to competition
(ii) to become aware once more of your kinaesthetic sense
(iii) to return to a point of balance
If you train yourself to relax momentarily and to withdraw at appropriate moments before or during competition, you will find your awareness and speed of reaction to be greatly increased when you focus on your performance again.

Gestalt therapy has a concept whose usefulness easily extends from a general social context to that of sport, and which shows the importance of knowing how to withdraw at the correct moment. In our social interaction a false sense of tact (usually a fear of disapproval) will keep us apparently attentive to those we are with long after we have lost interest so that we get stuck in a 'middle zone', somewhere between withdrawal and conscious social interaction. You can test this theory yourself by playing a simple game with two or three other athletes in which you say 'hello' when you feel yourself arrive fully present in a conversation, and 'goodbye' when you leave. You will find that you experience an unexpectedly heightened awareness during the moments when you are present.

When to relax

If you want to practise any of the 'deeper' methods of relaxation you would do best to choose a time after rather than before activity – after a hard training session, before your evening meal or before going to bed at night. Such relaxation is also particularly beneficial when you're tired, worried or unwell.

Relaxation that is 'momentary' or less profound can be used:

- *Before warming-up*
  We suggest that you begin your warm-up with some form of withdrawal or relaxation, however brief, to give you a sense of your own physical, emotional and mental state and a clear idea of what you need to do next. On those occasions where you feel over-anxious you should probably lengthen and deepen the process proportionately. The timing of it will vary from occasion to occasion, as indeed it does from athlete to athlete. Generally speaking, the less experienced you are at your sport and the more important the occasion, the nearer to the start of the competition should you do your relaxation.

- *When learning a new skill or tactic*
  Research shows that after a certain period of time the learning process peaks and that additional instruction or practice will confuse and undo the gains that have been made. If you intersperse periods of learning with periods of relaxation, you will absorb more in one session without deterioration of the learning process.

- *As a part of warming-down*
  Relax as a regular part of your warming-down procedure since it helps you return to a balanced physical state, reducing the risk of injury through non-release of tension.

- *Before practising any form of visualisation*
  Briefly relax before using visualisation techniques during competition. When practising visualisation before or after an event, begin with a relaxation that is somewhat deeper.

You may feel you can relax best by watching a film on the television or video at home. This might allow you to withdraw and release some physical and mental tension but if the film is exciting it will increase your emotional arousal and probably provoke physical and mental tensions of a different order. True relaxation gives a sense of distance from where you can watch your sensations, feelings and thoughts dispassionately as they arise and eventually learn from them.

There are a number of relaxation methods used in the West, many of which have been derived from Eastern yoga and other meditation techniques. Two of the better known are Autogenic Training, developed by the German Dr Schultz, and Progressive Relaxation developed by the American Dr Jacobsen. The first has been used to help patients with heart disease, high blood pressure, migraine headaches and other physical ills. A sequence of commands to the autonomic nervous system gradually teaches the patient to become aware of, and then gain control over, his breathing, heartbeat, body temperature and other hitherto uncontrolled parts of that system. Using this method, you can learn to raise and lower your arousal level at will.

Progressive Relaxation involves tensing each muscle group in turn, so that each group and the sense of tension in each group may be identified and released. As you expand your awareness of the difference between tension and release, you are increasingly able to release all your tension. In our *Sporting Bodymind* course we introduce a simpler method which emphasises the part played by breathing and the kinaesthetic sense of the body.

Relaxation exercises

You can reach the deeper states of relaxation more easily by lying down, but when your body is tired you are more likely to lose the quality of alertness in this position and drift towards sleep. This won't matter if you are relaxing to bring balance and rest after a demanding match or an exhausting day, but when you relax before a competition or before doing a visualisation exercise, it is best to sit with your back straight and supported. Eventually you can learn to relax in a standing position, taking two or three deep breaths, exhaling slowly and visualising your tension slipping to the ground like a heavy winter overcoat.

When sitting or standing, you should relax from your head downwards. When lying down it is best to relax from your feet upwards. It is easier for you to do the exercise if it is led by your coach, otherwise, even when you have learned the sequence and can visualise the soft tone of your coach's voice, you will be inclined to go too fast or to begin thinking about something else. If he leads the relaxation for the whole team, he should make sure that you all lie parallel to the same two walls with your feet about twenty inches apart, your hands twelve inches away from your sides, your arms straight, with no-one touching anyone else. If you haven't a coach, you could record or get someone else to record the instructions for you. The following examples of relaxation exercises should each take about ten minutes.

- 1 Close your eyes and adjust your position so that you are stretched out to make maximum contact with the ground, first raising and lowering your head to stretch your neck (making sure that your head is not tilted backwards), then wriggling to flatten your back and finally pushing away with your heels to stretch your legs.

  Take a deep breath and, as you let it out slowly: Feel the weight of your body on the ground . . . take another deep breath and let the ground begin to support your body . . . Take a moment to watch your feelings, as if you are standing out of doors on a clear night watching the moon . . . and imagine that the wisps of cloud floating by are like your feelings, watch them pass, identify them, give them a name . . .

  Now turn your attention to your thoughts and imagine that you are standing on a bridge, looking down at a stream, and your thoughts, whether statements, questions or pictures in your mind, are like leaves on the water passing under the bridge and away. Watch your thoughts and see them change . . .

  Now shift your attention back to your body. Notice again its weight . . . and become particularly aware of your feet. Notice the sensation of your toes, the muscles under your feet and around your ankles . . . if you find any tension there, stay with it and then a little while later, when exhaling, gradually let that tension go . . .

Allowing the floor to hold your feet, turn your attention to your calf muscles, feeling the bones of your lower legs, resting on your calf muscles with the muscles relaxed and supported by the floor . . .

Continue the relaxation at this pace, upwards through all the main muscle groups – thighs, groin, buttocks, pelvis, waist, stomach, lower back, upper back and chest, shoulders, upper arms, elbows, forearms, wrists, thumbs and hands, and let any remaining tension drain away through your fingers to the floor. Then pay attention to your neck, jaw, mouth, tongue, cheeks, muscles around your eyes, muscles of your eyes, of your forehead and over the crown of your head.

After a pause turn your attention once more to your feelings . . . to your thoughts . . . and then back to the weight of your body on the floor . . . Be aware of your toes, the muscles under your feet, your ankles . . .

And so on, running through the muscle groups from toes to head once more, much more quickly, just as a reminder, so you may release the last traces of tension.

Finally, notice the sensation of peacefulness and pleasure at having for a moment let go, allowed the floor to support your body . . . This is the 'death pose' in yoga, a position in which the body is as still as in death but in which you can feel the warmth and potential strength of life as your energy is replenished, knowing that you may move whenever you wish to move but choosing to enjoy this complete relaxation a little longer. . . . When you are ready . . . Stretch your arms over your head and slowly roll over on to one side and then sit up.

A sitting relaxation is conducted in the same way, with the muscle groups reversed and with instructions to allow the chair to gradually hold all the weight of your upper body, the floor to hold your legs and feet.

- 2 An alternative is to use a visualisation technique.

Imagine yourself as a shell, filled with a beautiful, heavy, coloured liquid . . . You have taps on your fingers and taps on your toes and as you are sitting a little man comes along and turns on the taps . . . and you can feel the liquid streaming out of the taps so that a clear space appears at the top of your head as the level gradually falls to your eyebrows, your eyes, your lips and down, down until the whole of your head is clear. The liquid has drained away from your neck and is leaving your shoulders, its weight pulling it smoothly down and away through your wrists, thumbs, hands and fingers . . . Now the whole of your upper body is clear and the remaining liquid is draining away through your pelvis, buttocks, the level dropping to your thighs, knees, ankles, feet and the last drops trickle away through your toes, leaving you empty, clear, light and relaxed, the shell of your body supported by the chair and the floor. . .

Concentration

What is concentration?

At the 1925 British Women's Golf Championships at Troon, Joyce Wethered holed a difficult putt on the eleventh green just as a train rumbled by. Later a friend asked how it was the train didn't disturb her. 'What train?' asked Joyce Wethered. Similarly, when Tony Jacklin worked with us in 1979, he spoke of his 'cocoon of concentration' as a state he experienced when playing his effortless best.

Concentration is a state of being that all sportspeople recognise as a prerequisite to good performance. It is an unwavering awareness of a specific subject to the momentary exclusion of other subjects. It may vary in intensity – not every golfer would be unaware of the train going by. Indeed, there are forms of 'deep' concentration as there are of 'deep' relaxation, many of them also stemming from Eastern disciplines such as meditation in its many forms (sitting meditations, slow movements like Tai Chi or the whirling meditations of the Dervishes), contemplation and prayer.

Concentration also varies in duration. The mesmeric quality of those first tennis finals between Bjorn Borg and John McEnroe was partly due to the striking difference in the style of concentration each had perfected. Borg's concentration did not seem to waver throughout the match, whilst McEnroe was able to shout at himself, query the umpire's decisions, seemingly lose touch completely with his objective and then snap back into his groove and serve a couple of effortless aces. McEnroe demonstrated the fallacy of the assumption that a short span of concentration is necessarily shallow.

John McEnroe and Bjorn Borg – two strikingly different but equally effective styles of concentration.

Concentration is a relaxed state of being alert, differing from anything held through will-power in that it *can* change its focus instantly to stay with the flow of competition. No relevant factors are shut out but the span of relevant factors at any given moment may narrow. Robert Nideffer, in an article in *Coach, Athlete and the Sports Psychologist* (edited by Peter Klavora, Juri Daniel, Univ. Toronto, 1979), differentiates between narrow and broad spans of concentration in terms of the *subject* of concentration. Aiming a dart at double-twenty on the darts board requires a narrow span of attention, whereas standing back to look at the score of your first two darts and calculating where the third dart must go requires a broad span. Nideffer also specifies a second dimension of concentration: internal and external. Internal concentration is focusing on your own sensations, feelings or thoughts. External concentration is focusing on subjects or events outside yourself. However, whatever the object of concentration, whether internal, external, narrow or broad (and both internal and external can be narrow *or* broad) the athlete with the deepest concentration is he who can harmonise the physical, emotional and mental strands of his being and focus them on the task at hand.

Why concentrate?

As an athlete, you need to maintain awareness of all the changing information relating to the run of competition, continually allowing the most relevant factor or factors to come into momentary focus at the expense of all else. Only then can you react instantly to full effect and achieve your goal.

Practising concentration can also teach you where your attention is really drawn and why it wants to go there. This is a valuable lesson which may eventually allow you to break long-held, outdated patterns of thought or behaviour. Eventually you become closely familiar with parts of your performance which are within your control and distanced from distractions or worries which stem from things that are beyond your control.

When to concentrate

- *During the event*
  The obvious answer is throughout the competition, but in fact many sports have alternate periods of activity and inactivity that demand continual change in the direction, span and intensity of your concentration. Discovering where best to focus your attention during periods of inactivity requires practice. Generally speaking, you should change your focus from external events to internal or vice versa, and from broad to narrow and back. This allows you to review the situation from different angles and gives you the chance to discover significant factors that you may have overlooked. It is also a way to recover and relax, a change indeed being 'as good as a rest'. You should however ensure that you do not get stuck in the 'middle zone', but either withdraw to an internal focus or go out and interact positively with the environment.

  Many distractions from the flow of play are centred on emotional considerations: who is in the crowd, fear of injury, or the prospect of a difficult encounter later in the day. The next section gives suggestions for dealing with this problem.

■ *Before and after the event*
You can perform most concentration exercises at home, prior to the match as part of your warm-up, or during a break in your performance. However, as with relaxation and visualisation, most of the exercises are best learned and first practised away from the competitive situation.

How to concentrate

To a great extent you can improve your concentration through carefully-devised technical and tactical training sessions. Once your coach (or indeed you yourself) has identified occasions where you habitually become distracted, you can focus your training on those particular situations, creating exercises which demand longer and more intense periods of concentration than the competition itself. This may be enough. However, just as weight-training can provide a very specific type of exercise to increase physical strength and stamina and has the added advantage that it fits in easily to your own routine as additional training, so certain other physical and mental exercises allow you to work intensively to improve your concentration.

The first step towards making a change is to discover where your attention goes when it drifts away. Does your mind go to factors in the environment that are outside your performance or does it go to your past or future experience? Once again, recognising your patterns is the first step towards making a change.

The change can be made by:

■ *Building and practising a stronger pattern*
This means establishing some kind of ritual such as:
(i) adopting the six-point warming-up procedure described in chapter 1
(ii) choosing and practising a number of task-oriented thought patterns to use if distractions threaten once the event has started. You could for instance plan to return your attention to your breathing (an internal focus) at breaks during the competition or you could focus on some factor that is an integral part of the competition – the wave ahead or the feel of the rudder (in the case of sailing)

■ *Strengthening the attraction of the object or action on which you want to focus*
Almost any chosen task would do here, such as seeing how high the tennis ball is each time it crosses the net or feeling exactly where your weight might be each time you hit the ball.

■ *Deliberately paying attention to the distraction*
This means treating it as if it has a life of its own, giving it space, discovering its needs and eventually making a contract to deal with it later. You might use the *black box* technique described in chapter 1.

■ *Making friends with the distraction*
This may mean practising in an environment in which these distractions are simulated or it may mean finding a way to view the distraction positively. Poet Laureate John Betjeman once confessed that he used to hate traffic in general and lorries in particular. 'I took such a dislike to them that I bought a little book to tell me their names. It was the only way to get to not to mind them.' he said.

When we held a course at a sports centre within earshot of three squash courts, it helped to consider ourselves part of the same community as the squash players, all of us benefitting from use of the building in our own ways. We might also have welcomed the noise as a chance to practise the concentration technique about which we were talking at the time!

■ *Removing focus from emotional distractions to physical and mental patterns*
Breathing deeply and allowing yourself to relax and possibly visualising yourself in a *quiet place* (see p. 94).

■ *Removing focus from physical or mental distractions to emotional patterns*
In team sports, for instance, team spirit provides a powerful focus for agreed action and a few well-chosen words of emotional contact between you and your team mates or you and your coach will direct your individual as well as your collective concentration towards success.

Concentration exercises

1 Sit in an upright chair, with both feet on the ground and arms uncrossed. Close your eyes, take a deeper breath and let it out slowly as you begin to relax from the forehead downwards . . . Once you are relaxed, notice your breathing and, without changing its rhythm, begin to count silently so that one breath (in and out again) counts as one, the next in and out breath counts as two, and so on. When you reach ten, go back to one and start again. If you lose count or find yourself counting beyond ten, stop and trace your wandering thoughts back as far as you can before you start again at one. To begin with about eight minutes of this exercise will be enough.

2 Sit in an upright chair and place some object or photograph related to your sport in front of you. Relax as before but keep your eyes open. Spend five minutes without moving, noticing as many qualities of that object as you can.

3 This is a similar exercise, but this time you sit with pencil and paper and write down the name of an object from your sport in the centre of the page. Enclose the word in a circle and then, using the circle like the hub of a wheel, draw out a 'spoke' with a word at its end, denoting an

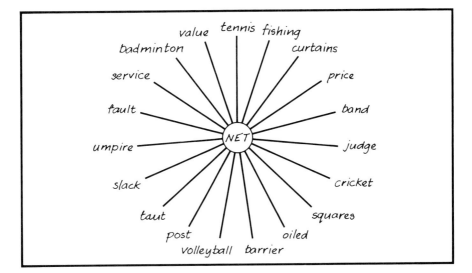

object or quality that you connect for a moment with the circled word. Then go back to the circled word and let another connection come, drawing out another 'spoke' of the wheel with the new word at its end. Repeat this process until you have a complete 'wheel' of words surrounding the original one.

4 This is another breathing exercise which involves choosing an 'affirmation' (a short positive sentence, see p. 86) as the focus of attention. Place the index finger of your left hand on the forehead at a point just above and between your eyebrows, your thumb against the left nostril to close it and then with eyes closed breathe in through the right nostril for the count of four. Then let your middle finger close your right nostril and, holding your breath, say the affirmation silently. Then take your thumb away and breathe out of the left nostril to the count of four. Then breathe in to the count of four through the left, close the left nostril, hold, and repeat the affirmation, release the right and breathe out through the right to the count of four. Repeat this sequence five times.

5 Shuttling – this is a gestalt exercise designed to help you to avoid getting stuck in the 'middle zone'. Work with a partner. If you go first, close your eyes and tune in to some sensation, feeling or thought and say: 'Now I am aware of a pain in my leg.' or 'Now I am aware of my breathing.' or 'Now I am feeling silly.' etc. Then open your eyes and say 'Now I am aware . . .' adding something that is happening *outside* yourself. For instance, 'Now I am aware of the sunlight.' or 'Now I am aware of your eyes.' etc. Repeat the process – first an inside statement, then an outside one – for a few minutes without a break. (If you get stuck your partner should prompt you by asking: 'Now I am aware . . .?' thereby hauling you back out of the 'middle zone'.) Then let your partner do the same. Later you can try the exercise with your eyes open all the time.

6 We normally teach one concentration exercise that involves slow movement, physical control and balance in our *Sporting Bodymind* courses and a number of athletes from various sports, including weight-lifting, sailing and tennis now practise it regularly. This is as follows:

Stand in a relaxed position, with your hands by your sides and your feet together. Slowly lift your left foot up and outwards, bent at the knee. Then bring it as far as possible across your body without turning at the waist. At the same time slowly lift your hands to a 'twenty-to-four' position away from your body. Without stopping, bring your leg back across your body and then round behind you, bending slowly forwards, stretching your hands in front of you and your leg behind until your body is parallel to the ground.

Then reverse the movement . . . bring the left leg back round in front of your body once more and then back in the same arc until you put your foot gently back on the ground, your hands meantime having returned to your sides. Without a break, repeat the movement with your right leg, this time balancing on your left.

The second part of the exercise follows a different sequence. This time lift your left leg, bent at the knee, straight in front of you till you can hold your ankle, then still holding your ankle bend gradually down and put your foot back on the ground. Then let go of the ankle and, still bent forwards, transfer your hands slowly to the right ankle, straighten up, holding your right ankle, lower it to the ground again, transfer your hands to hold your left ankle again, straighten up and then let go and slowly lower your left foot back to the ground.

Both parts of the exercise should be done smoothly and very slowly indeed.

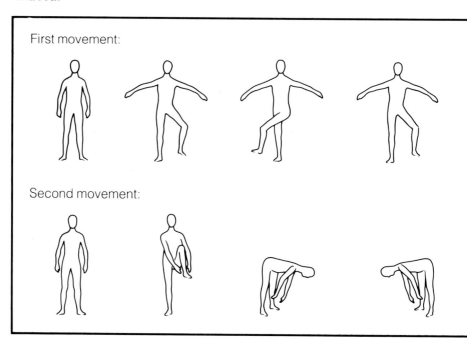

First movement:

Second movement:

Key Points

RELAXATION	CONCENTRATION

RELAXATION

- appropriate level varies from individual to individual and occasion to occasion.
- complete relaxation regenerates and allows recognition of resources, patterns of behaviour and environment.
- momentary relaxation increases speed of reaction, restores balance and gives awareness of kinaesthetic sense.

Use relaxation
- before warming up.
- when learning a new skill or tactic.
- as a part of warming down.
- before practising any form of visualisation.

Relaxation techniques
- autogenic training.
- progressive relaxation.
- *Sporting Bodymind* method, –
- when lying down.
- when sitting or standing (with visualisation).

CONCENTRATION

- allows you to react instantly, to full effect.
- brings familiarity with parts of performance within your control and distance from parts outside your control.
- helps break down out-dated patterns within your performance.

Use concentration
- during event, varying depth, duration, direction and span, according to situation.
- before and after event, through exercises to improve ability.

Deal with loss of concentration by
- building and practising strong patterns of behaviour.
- strengthening the attraction of the object or action on which you want to focus.
- deliberately paying attention to the distraction.
- 'making friends' with the distraction.
- removing focus from emotional distraction to physical and mental patterns.
- removing focus from mental or physical distractions to emotional patterns.
- practising concentration exercises.

Follow the sequence as indicated then reverse the action without putting your leg back on the ground. Now, without pausing, repeat the sequence with your right leg.

4
VISUALISATION

When you daydream about the putt you sank on the fourteenth green or remember how that passing shot on the tennis court felt as you broke your opponent's service at four–four in the second set, your 'thinking' is visual or felt, rather than something that happens in words.

Consciously or unconsciously, we are all adept at visual thinking. However, the step from visual thinking to visualisation is similar to the step from natural sporting ability to sophisticated technical and tactical skill. Like any physical skill, the ability to create powerful mental imagery needs to be taught and practised regularly if it's going to improve your performance.

In this chapter we describe various mental rehearsal techniques that can help you: increase your confidence; speed up the process of learning a new skill; change a bad habit; and improve the consistency of your performance.

What is visualisation?

Visualisation is a skill. It is the process of watching yourself on a screen in your mind's eye, consciously evoking and guiding daydreams in which you appear, usually towards a specific end. Something may be happening to you or you may be moving in a particular way. Usually (but not always) you visualise with your eyes closed so that distracting signals are blocked out.

The academic term for this technique is 'mental imaging'. We keep the common usage 'visualisation', but it is important to remember that visualisation includes an auditory and a kinaesthetic (feeling) component. In other words, if you visualise yourself moving, you may see, hear and feel yourself moving. *In most visualisation, the kinaesthetic sense is particularly important.*

Maxi Gnauck from East Germany mentally rehearsing her technique while chalking-up for her asymmetric bars routine.

Why visualise?

How will imagining yourself serving against an opponent in tennis or spiking a ball down the line in volleyball improve your performance of the skill? How will visualising a crucial chip from a bare lie really help you cope with a tight situation on the seventeenth in your club's medal competition? Does imagining yourself relaxing really help?

In fact, simply *watching* a player with a certain style and technique can rub off on an impressionable player sometimes for better, sometimes for worse. Matts Wilander, the youngest ever winner of the French Open and a countryman of Bjorn Borg, was interviewed by a television reporter before his big win at the Stade Roland Garros in 1982. When the reporter tried to draw analogies between his style of play and Borg's, Wilander pointed out that *all* Swedish youngsters used a two-handed backhand and heavy topspin. For a while the whole nation of young tennis players unconsciously emulated Borg, resulting in a promising crop of young players. In Britain, it has long been recognised that the standard of public court tennis improves markedly during the period of the Wimbledon championships because of the impact of television.

Since it is equally true that watching a bad player uncritically or replaying your mistakes mentally can have a *negative* effect on your performance, it is important that you begin to gain control over the images that travel through your mind. Ray Clemence, the England and Spurs goalkeeper, almost drove into a line of traffic cones on his way home after losing one disastrous match. 'I couldn't get the match out of my head,' he said, 'I kept seeing those goals I let in.' This was negative visual thinking – a vivid, anguished daydream. Mental rehearsal, the class of visualisation we describe here, is the technique of controlling these images of physical performance to positive effect. There are three reasons why this is so effective.

It affects physical functioning

Visualisation of a physical action, process or state can affect your physical reality, as can visualisation of an emotional state. When you imagine yourself moving, the muscle groups involved in such an action actually move on a subliminal level. When visualising, you send small messages through your nervous system to those muscles. Research conducted in the 1930s by Dr Edmund Jacobson demonstrated that when an individual imagined tensing and then relaxing a muscle group, he could learn to influence that muscle group without doing any actual tensing or relaxing. In the last twenty years, research into biofeedback techniques has demonstrated our ability to change bloodpressure, rate of heartbeat, body temperature and a variety of hitherto 'involuntary' functions of the body.

It helps to accelerate the learning process

The second reason for the importance of visualisation lies in the fact that, although skills such as fielding a line drive in baseball or sinking a free throw shot in basketball are physical, all the organisation and co-ordination of movement takes place in the brain. The whole purpose of practising a skill is to tell the brain, as accurately and clearly as possible, how to organise the movement of the body. It is in the brain where the ultimate learning of skills, as well as the unlearning of bad habits, takes place.

A simple way of picturing this is to imagine that your brain resembles the road system of a city like London. London, unlike New York, for example, was never planned from the start. As the city grew and spread, however, travellers in and out of Greater London slowly developed a system for getting from one place to any other, finding the shortest and quickest routes, so that all of the villages and towns became connected. The city planners, recognising this, introduced wider streets, more systematic stop lights, paved the roads and sometimes even set up one-way systems.

Similarly, in sport, when you practise and practise a skill, you are running signals to your muscles from the brain and back, 'clearing' and 'widening' those nervous pathways, clearly marking connections and intersections so that there will be the minimum of delay in translating the signals and co-ordinating movement.

Mental rehearsal can help short cut the learning process and complement the actual physical practice of skills. It allows you to travel the pathways and make the connections, emphasising specific aspects of the skill where necessary. Visualisation may also be used to gain information which might otherwise be lost from the body. You can tap your nervous system's memory in a way which is not possible through analysis.

It uses a language understood by the body

Because so much of our education and training involves analysis and verbal communication, we forget that these ways of thinking are only abstractions of experiences which happen on the level of sensations. If you were asked to describe your golf swing in as much detail as possible, you could probably write several pages of detailed analysis. If you are a golf professional, you could probably write a book! However, anyone who has ever coached a sport knows how frustrating it can be to try to teach someone a skill verbally. This is particularly the case if you are trying to change a well-grooved bad habit.

To illustrate this at a *Sporting Bodymind* course, we conduct an exercise in which one person stands on a chair with his eyes closed whilst a second person tells him how to get down. One of two things happens: either the person steps down immediately, in which case he is probably getting down the way he would habitually and is not really listening to the instructions; or the exercise takes several minutes as the instructor imagines what it feels like making the movement in order to break it down into its components and translate it into words. When we give signals to the body, these signals are best received in a language that the body understands: a language which uses the body's sensations (feeling, seeing, hearing, smell, temperature, colour, movement, etc.) as its main vocabulary.

Types of visualisation: the two classes

Different situations call for different types of visualisation. We draw a distinction between two main classes of visualisation – *'problem solving'* and *'mental rehearsal'* – each of which uses several different techniques.

'Problem solving' involves using visualisation to aid concentration, to reduce anxiety and physical tension, or to suggest possible courses of action. Imagining putting distractions into a box or tension draining like liquid from your body are two 'problem solving' visualisations we've already described. Other techniques of this kind are mentioned in chapters 6 and 7.

'Mental rehearsal', the second class, is the process of imagining yourself performing a specific movement or skill. There are five mental rehearsal techniques: *performance practice* (of which there are five types): *instant preplay, during performance* or *'As if . . .'*, *instant replay* and *performance review*. We describe these later, but first here are a few guidelines as to how you can best learn to visualise.

How to visualise

Some athletes take longer than others to learn to visualise effectively but most enjoy the process. It is much easier if you have someone to help you set up your programme and to lead you through your visualisation from time to time. Leading a visualisation – helping the athlete to relax, giving appropriate instructions, asking the right questions and noticing significant expressions – is also a skill. It isn't difficult for a coach to learn this skill but many *team* coaches, without changing their priorities, don't have enough time. This is one situation in which having a sports psychologist on the coaching staff is an advantage.

The following guidelines will improve the quality and effectiveness of the exercise, whether you are practising alone or with someone else.

Useful guidelines

- *Start with a relaxation*
  If you are learning a new skill, or even practising an old one, well-timed periods of relaxation will promote more rapid progress. This is particularly the case with any form of mental rehearsal. Since you are asking your highly tuned nervous system to organise subtle and often new information, it is important not to send that system a hodgepodge of conflicting signals.

  A dialogue is going on between your brain and body during mental rehearsal. Since mental rehearsal takes place on a more subtle level than physical practice, it is important that you don't have to override conflicting 'static' from physical tension. Such tension will clog the communication channels between mind and body. A preliminary relaxation allows the conversation to take place as clearly as possible.

Morris Strode, U.S.A. – visualising between sets. (See also page 94).

■   *Stay alert*
    Both relaxation *and* concentration are needed to visualise successfully,
    concentration making the images stronger. Concentration also allows
    clearer signals and gives more information about any skill you are
    visualising. Discover what your concentration abilities are and don't
    demand more of your attention span than it can give. You may
    alternate relaxation and visualisation for three minutes, five minutes or
    as much as ten minutes, but not more. Should you discover that your
    concentration is wavering repeatedly, end the session and make sure
    that your next sessions are shorter.

Most visualisation (certainly all mental rehearsal) should be done sitting rather than lying down. If you lie down your mind will be more inclined to wander and you may fall asleep.

- *Use the present tense*
When you recount your visualisation, you should speak in the present tense, as should the person listening and asking questions. This makes the visualisation more vivid.

- *Set realistic goals*
Choose goals which are within your reach. While it is fun to imagine that you are the world's number one golfer, six times consecutive winner at Wimbledon or the modern-day Pele of the soccer pitch, this kind of mental rehearsal (called the *ideal model visualisation*) has value only under certain specific conditions. Normally, you should imagine yourself performing at a level of high proficiency but one which you know you can and occasionally do reach. As your physical proficiency increases, so should the performance that you visualise, but always maintain some correspondence between your performance in competition and your mental rehearsal practice.

We remember some years ago teaching mental rehearsal to a golfer with a handicap of ten. He had particular difficulty making short chips on to the green. He was always underswinging and watching the ball dribble up to the edge of the green or else overswinging and watching the ball fly away over the other side. When he worked through a mental rehearsal, we focused on his kinaesthetic sense of performing an accurate chip. A week or two later he arrived for another session. 'It's not working,' he said. Asked why not and he replied, 'Well, I can visualise it all perfectly but when I *play* I'm not sinking my chips.' Somewhat surprised, we asked 'But you were visualising yourself making a *good* chip. Surely you weren't seeing it bounce once and go into the hole?' 'Well, yes,' he said somewhat sheepishly, 'you *did* tell me I should *enjoy* mental rehearsal.'

One further caution. Be aware that when you focus your attention entirely on goals, rather than the process or means whereby the goals are achieved, whether in physical training or mental rehearsal, you are making a fundamental mistake. It is only when you are in touch with a wide and broad experience of what you are doing to achieve the goal that the goal will in fact be achieved. Then you achieve it as a matter of course.

- *Set specific goals*
Your goals in mental rehearsal should complement those of your normal physical practice. When you choose the skill you want to improve, make it *specific*. Is it your backhand or forehand? Are you at the net, in the middle of the court or on the baseline? Are you moving into position or are you set and waiting for the ball to reach you? Make it even more specific. Who are you playing? Which part of the court are you aiming for? Is it a power shot or are you placing the ball

delicately? The more specific you make the visual and kinaesthetic image, the more effect it will have.

Furthermore, by making your visualisation so specific, you can determine in which aspects of your game you are competent and on which you need to focus during your physical training. Mental rehearsal and your skills training are intimately related. Each can be used to give you insight into what needs practising in the other. When your skill level falls, go back to a mental rehearsal of a perfect shot. If you can't imagine the perfect shot, you are probably performing that shot differently each time and have no 'feel' for how it should be. Then you must watch someone else again. When you can mentally rehearse the skill perfectly and have recovered physically, go back on court and practise again.

■ *Use all your senses*
You should particularly use the visual, auditory and kinaesthetic senses. Sir Francis Galton was the first to realise that different people respond better to an exchange of ideas and information when it is phrased in different sensory language. Notice how your friends and fellow athletes talk. One will say 'From the sound of it, the best approach is to . . .' Another will say 'The way I see it we should . . .' And a third might say 'I've got a feeling that we should . . .' Each person is expressing their experience of the same situation in terms of a different sense, the primary ones being seeing, hearing and feeling. When you visualise you may notice that your sense of sound is stronger than your kinaesthetic sense, or that your kinaesthetic feeling of an activity is stronger than your visual image. You may find colours and images are vivid, but have problems *feeling* what you are doing.

It is normal for you to have a primary sense and two secondary ones. These vary from person to person. Thus, the first step in mental rehearsal is to identify which sense is the strongest. Which one are you most comfortable with when describing your inner experience of an event? Begin there. Then as you progress through your mental rehearsals you will be able to add the other senses and begin to make full use of your visualisation abilities.

A young athlete who is made to specialise too early in his career risks the danger of limiting his abilities and his way of thinking about his sport. If, as a soccer player, you are always thinking defensively you won't know what to do with the ball when you find yourself in a scoring position. When you specialise too soon as a forward, you may not be able to tackle an opponent at a crucial moment. Furthermore, you will have difficulty anticipating the movements of your team mates and opponents because of your limited experience of the game. The same is true of mental rehearsal. Introduce all three senses as soon as it is comfortable to do so.

We even encourage athletes to include their sense of taste and smell in their mental imagery. These appear periodically and may be important. Gymnasts respond immediately to the imagined taste of chalk. It is an important sensory clue for making the scene more real to their imagination. When leading a golfer through a mental rehearsal, we asked him 'What hole are you on now in this approach shot?' 'The fifteenth' he replied immediately. Impressed by his prompt response we asked 'How do you know?' 'Because there is a farmer who keeps pigs just the other side of the out of bounds!' he said.

Create as real a sensory impression of the sporting situation as possible. Include every detail of the actual situation that you can remember. The stronger the sensory component and the more realistic the visualisation, the more powerful the message to your nervous system. The more powerful the message, the more effective the mental rehearsal will be in organising your nervous system to respond *during your sports performance.*

When leading a yachtsman through his first mental rehearsal, we felt that the picture wasn't complete. 'What else can you add to the scene?' We asked 'The light? the weather? some sounds?' 'No,' he said smiling, his eyes still closed, 'I can taste the salt on my lips.'

■   *Visualise from the inside out and from the outside in*
One of the first things to surface when we teach mental rehearsal is that some people watch themselves acting from a slight distance, whilst others feel themselves acting from the inside looking out. Both ways of mental imaging are valid. If you are 'on the outside' watching yourself, you are probably more visually oriented, whereas if you are 'inside' looking out you are probably more kinaesthetically oriented. We suggest that to begin with you should follow your natural inclination and visualise in whichever way is easiest. When you have practised the mental rehearsal effectively from that perspective, you can try the other way.

That said, it is our experience that the kinaesthetic sense must be included in mental rehearsal if the most powerful impression on the nervous system is to be made. Since sport is essentially a physical, kinaesthetic and kinetic activity, mental rehearsal where you are on the inside feeling yourself perform will create a sensory impression which is closest to the way you feel when you are actually performing your sport.

The visual component has a complementary use. Sometimes, when you are doing something wrong and can't work out what needs changing, stepping outside and watching yourself will give you a visual picture of what you are doing and can provide that crucial insight to spot the problem area. It may sound strange but it works.

■   *Visualise at the correct speed*
Generally speaking, if mental rehearsal is to improve your perform- ance, it must be practised at the same speed as you would practise the skills you are visualising. If you rehearse something slower, that is indeed what you are practising. Mental rehearsal should replicate the performance situation, with the same playing conditions, such as speed of movement, objects, colours, climate.

However, there are two occasions when you should slow your mental rehearsal down. The first is when you set up the rehearsal programme. This should be done with your coach or team mate who will ask you to relate the sequence of movements, and will question you to ensure that the sequence is technically correct. This procedure is particularly important when your objective is to reinforce your learning of a new skill or a new way of performing that skill. Slowing the sequence down will help you to get a full and complete sense of what goes into the movement. When you have that complete sensory picture, you can rehearse at normal speed. We recommend that you finish *any* mental rehearsal with a repetition at the correct speed.

The other situation in which it is appropriate to slow down your mental rehearsal is when you are trying to break a bad habit or change your technique. Slowing the visualisation down then allows you to isolate those components of your technique which are detracting from your performance in that aspect of your game. Take the movement apart, slow it down, change the parts you know are limiting your performance, substitute more appropriate action and then play it through at the proper speed in the new way.

We seldom suggest that you rehearse at speeds *faster* than those at which the actual event takes place.

■ *Practise regularly*
Consistency is more important than length of rehearsal. A patchy pattern of practice does little good. If possible, practise your visualisations at the same time and for the same length of time each day. If you have a particular room or place which is quiet and where you won't be disturbed, use it regularly. Of course, there are many times when you won't be able to use the same place. If you end up having to practise on the way to a match or in the bath at night it is better than missing your rehearsal completely.

Five to ten minutes a day for five to six days a week is a good rhythm, particularly at the beginning. Three minutes a day, five days a week, is much more effective than twenty minutes one day, five minutes the next and none the third. It is best to moderate a first rush of enthusiasm and a feeling that you want to practise 30 minutes a day. Not only may you fail to be consistent but frequent short spells of visualisation would be more effective. We suggest that to begin with you rehearse for a minute, then take a deep breath, let it out slowly and relax for thirty seconds, repeat the rehearsal, relax and repeat the sequence four or five times.

■ *Enjoy it!*
Mental rehearsal should be enjoyable. If you are getting bored or frustrated, stop or change your programme to a different aspect of your game. Remember that when you are relaxed and engaged in visual thinking, you are open to negative as well as positive thoughts and feelings. It doesn't make sense to introduce negative thoughts, frustrations or anxiety into your mental pictures of your sport. Were you to do so, they would inevitably spill over into your actual performance, which would then suffer.

Mental rehearsal techniques

Introductory exercise

Here is an undemanding exercise to help you to visualise with all of your senses. Sit as comfortably as possible and close your eyes. Take a moment to relax. Take a few deep breaths . . . and let yourself imagine, one after another, the following sensory experiences:

A sunset over the ocean . . . white clouds racing over the sky . . . a piece of sports equipment you use regularly . . . a famous player in your sport . . . the face of a friend . . . a building which you like . . . a rose as it opens and blooms.

Now imagine . . .
The sound of a rainstorm on a tin roof . . . church bells ringing in the distance . . . the roar of a crowd after a home team has scored an important point . . . the sound of wind in the trees . . . a favourite piece of music . . . the voice of a team mate or person you often play against.

Now imagine . . .
The feel of the sun on your back on a hot day . . . jumping into a hot bath or shower . . . jumping into a cold bath or shower . . . tightening the laces of your sport shoes on each foot in turn . . . the grasp of a firm handshake . . . running over a grassy field.

Now imagine . . .
The smell of burning leaves . . . the smell of a changing room . . . the smell of bacon cooking on the stove . . . the smell of a new piece of equipment or clothing.

Now imagine . . .
The taste of the bacon you just cooked . . . the taste of a fresh piece of fruit . . . the salty taste of sweat . . . the taste of a cool refreshing drink after physical exercise.

Before completing this imaging, take a moment to reflect on which sense was the easiest to evoke. Which one was the most difficult? This will give you an idea of which sense is the primary one for you and which ones are secondary.

Then close your eyes again and take a moment to imagine yourself performing your sport. You may be performing a particular move or a sequence of moves. You may be practising or performing in a competition. This doesn't matter but as you perform take a moment to notice which factors perceived by each sense – visual (seeing); auditory (hearing); kinaesthetic (feeling); olfactory (smelling); gustatory (tasting) – seem significant.

When you have finished, open your eyes and take a few moments to write these factors down. The list you make will be important. These will be powerful cues and essential associations you have with your sport. Evoking these associations will be a valuable aid not only for mental rehearsal but also when preparing for competition. Before you can use the most supportive conditions in your environment, or put

Mark Blencarne, England – on his way to winning the gold medal at the 1982 Commonwealth Games.

○ aside the most distracting, you must first become fully aware of them.
○ So keep your list and add to it as you notice each new element and the
○ influence it has on you.

Performance practice

This is normally done at home and involves visualising the performance of a specific skill that you want to develop or improve. It complements your physical practice of the skill and becomes part of your daily routine, as physical training sessions are a part of your regular week. The technique can increase your confidence and speed the process of learning a new skill. Practising it in relaxed circumstances can often provide the key to changing a bad habit as well as improving the consistency of your performance.

Given that technique and form are in great measure dependent on a precise mental co-ordination, this type of visualisation is also invaluable when physical practice is impossible through injury, bad weather or other circumstances. The continuity of a *performance practice* routine need not be interrupted by sickness or injury. Your nervous system then remains tuned in to the skills of your sport and you regain your form much faster when you are fit enough to practise again physically.

An American horsewoman on one of our courses explained that she used mental rehearsal of her dressage performance to supplement the physical practice she did with her horse. Finding she needed more practice than the horse (who began to anticipate her signals or become jaded through over practice if she did all of her own practice physically), she continued her practice of posture, form and alignment through mental rehearsal.

Occasionally the *performance practice* technique may be used at the place where you perform. Some athletes like to include it in their process of warming-up. Some coaches will ask athletes to end a training session with a mental rehearsal of the skill they had been practising to eliminate the memory of any final repetitions that had been below par because of fatigue.

If the demands of your sport require you to reduce physical training during the few days immediately prior to competition, you can increase the frequency of your *performance practice* rehearsal, whilst broadening its scope to include all you know about the place where the competition is to be held. However, a five-minute practice each day, which includes relaxation, would otherwise be enough until you want, and have the commitment, to do more. When you have that commitment it is better to increase the number rather than the duration of your practices

There are five different kinds of *performance practice*, which are described here in exercise form.

● 1 *Basic performance practice exercise*
○ Sit down in a place where you will not be disturbed. Uncross your legs
○ and arms. Close your eyes and relax from your head downwards.
○ See yourself in a place where you can practise the skill that you want
○ to improve. Create as real and genuine a scene as possible. Where is it?
○ Is it indoors or out? If indoors, how high is the ceiling? What sort of
○ lighting is there? Can you hear ventilation fans? Are people watching?

If outdoors, what is the season, the time of day, the weather? What colours do you see? What clothes are people wearing? What smells are there? What sounds do you hear? See and sense as much detail as possible.

Suddenly, as you watch, you see yourself walk into the picture and begin to prepare for practice. If you are holding some piece of equipment, notice your grip. How do you prepare yourself to perform? Watch carefully.

Then you begin to practise the skill. Notice particularly those critical factors which are the cutting edge of your ability and which you are going to improve. See yourself performing really well. Where do you initiate the movement? How is your balance? How do you use your arms and head? How do you use your legs? Your hips? Notice as much detail as possible.

Then go back to the beginning. Take a moment to settle down and watch yourself perform the activity once more, aware of all of its details. Then stop. Take a deep breath, letting it out slowly as you go back to your visualisation. Change your position so that you can watch the same scene from somewhere else – from a different side, closer or further away.

From this new vantage point, watch the same performance. Notice as many good elements as possible. Don't force it but coax the image from your memory. If part of the image is vague don't worry. If it is clear, notice what new insights you get by watching from this angle. If the action is brief, play it through a couple more times. Then come back to the room and without opening your eyes take another deeper breath. As you let it out slowly, let yourself release any new or remaining tension before returning to your visualisation.

This time, as you begin your performance, focus your attention on one of your hands. Watch closely . . . and you suddenly realise that you are now watching from *inside* your body and you can *feel* yourself complete the movement. Before starting again, take a moment to feel the weather through your skin. Notice the touch of your clothes. Notice what parts of your body seem most alive. Look around. What do you see? What objects and colours do you notice? What sounds do you hear? What can you smell?

Now prepare to practise the skill again and as you move be aware of all the sensations and feelings you identify with a perfect action. Notice how good it feels. Again, if your action is brief, repeat it a couple of times.

Finally, after another moment's relaxation, repeat the action with your awareness focused on one element of the movement. This might be a part of your technique with which you have had difficulty in the past or a specific area of the body which you have previously ignored. Notice how this element of the movement or part of the body functions when you perform with the grace and ease of your visualisation. Let yourself enjoy the sense of integration as you run through the movement once more.

Before you end the exercise, let your attention expand again into your whole body so that you are as conscious as possible of how you feel. Notice that the end product flows from the sensation of performing the activity efficiently and gracefully, that this sensation is itself the key.

2 *The ideal model*

This is the first of four variations on *performance practice*, all of which follow the same basic format.

Kinaesthetic imagery will improve with practice but, if parts of the *basic performance practice* visualisation were completely blank, either the skill you were practising is incompletely learned or you have no consistent way of performing it. This next exercise should help. It's one which invariably gives pleasure and will frequently provide some new insight into your performance.

Think of an athlete who performs the skill you are trying to improve perfectly – either a senior athlete in your own club or someone you've watched often on television. Be sure that his or her style doesn't clash with yours. Not many golfers would want to imitate Aoki's swing. You may also want to choose someone of much the same height and weight as yourself: an épéeist with a six-inch longer reach than you will fence differently.

Settle into your chair, with your eyes closed and run through your relaxation. Then feel yourself back at the place where you were practising the skill but this time, instead of watching yourself, you are watching your 'ideal model'. As he begins to perform the skill that you are wanting to practise, notice how he uses his body in as much detail as possible.

Watch him a couple of times, relax again and repeat the rehearsal, this time focusing on one of the athlete's hands as he starts the movement again . . . realise that it is *your* hand and you have *become* that athlete, and *feel* what it is like to move in that way. Be aware of the ease, the strength, the confidence and pleasure of performing like this and after two or three rehearsals, bring these feelings back with you to the room.

We carried out this exercise to good effect with an English tennis player on the international women's circuit who was aware that she needed to improve her running to one side to make a passing shot, but that it was particularly difficult to practise this movement in training. Asked which player she thought best at this shot, she had a clear picture of Ivan Lendl. We then did an *ideal model* rehearsal in which she first saw Lendl performing this shot and then she 'became' Lendl and acquired the kinaesthetic feeling of playing this way. Asked what she could feel that was different to the way she usually played, she said 'I start running earlier, I'm in control with my feet and I use my right foot as a break.' This rehearsal became an exercise she could practise to fill in the gap in her training.

3 *Top performance visualisation*

This varies from the *basic performance practice* exercise in that you practise a skill you know *you* have performed perfectly in the past. You should have no difficulty visualising this performance but if your present level of skill is no longer as high as it was, you are likely to discover some basic differences. For example, a rugby player, rehearsing an occasion when he ran more aggressively with the ball, might notice in his visualisation that his stride was longer then than it is now. This gives him an indication of how he may regain his form.

As you go through the visualisation, watch yourself from first one position and then another, noticing which aspect of your technique is the key to the total performance. Then move into yourself and play the rehearsal through again, focusing particularly on this key aspect and notice how it *feels* to perform in this way. If there was more than one important aspect, run through the inner version of the visualisation again, focusing on the sensations of each aspect in turn. Then finish the exercise with one more rehearsal, aware of the pleasure and confidence of performing the action so well, bringing this feeling back with you to the room.

4 *Right place/right time*
This exercise also involves visualisation of a perfect action performed at some past event but is not designed to improve a particular skill. Rather, it is designed to put you back in touch with the general feeling of performing perfectly well.

First, relax, and, to ensure that your mind and emotions are quiet, you might run through the *black box* exercise.

Now visualise yourself settling back into the chair, looking out of the window, let the scene change and evoke the memory of a moment in your sports career when you felt you were in the right place at the right time . . . just one such moment, the first that occurs to you, a moment when you could do no wrong, when you seemed to know in advance what was going to happen, when it seemed some part of you was a dispassionate observer.

Notice what you are doing, where you are and who you are with, but above all notice what it *feels* like to perform in this way. Play through the short sequence that came to you spontaneously, then repeat it twice more focusing on the natural balanced flow of your action and then come back to the room and open your eyes.

5 *Substitution rehearsal*
If you are unable to perfect the mental rehearsal of a skill, no matter how hard you practise, you may be focusing on the very errors that you are trying to eliminate. One way of dealing with this is to go back to seeing yourself perform a *different* skill in a different situation perfectly and then to make a gradual transition until you eventually see this competent self performing the problem skill.

Having relaxed, set the scene and watch your competent self practise a skill with ease and grace. Step into this self and experience the feeling of performing this way. The feeling is all-important so spend a moment soaking it up – then go back to an observer's position and

watch this competent self as he performs the problem skill. What
stands out about the way he uses his body? How is he balanced?
How is his timing? What new approach is he taking to this problem
shot? What part of his body is working differently?

Replay the sequence from one or two different observation points,
noticing the key differences again and then, after another relaxation,
regain the feeling of *being* the competent self. Come back to the
opening scene and finish the rehearsal by playing the problem shot
through from inside with this confident, competent feeling, paying
particular attention to the key aspects that you noted previously.

Having finished the rehearsal, write down those key aspects and go
out and practise the skill physically. Feel and practise these changes in
your physical performance and notice which are particularly effective.
Later that day practise the *substitution rehearsal* again repeating the
process for a few days until you find it easy to imagine the competent
you taking over and practising the difficult skill. Eventually you will
have begun to piece together a new response to the problem shot and
will be able to use a *basic performance practice* rehearsal for further
training.

Instant preplay

This kind of mental rehearsal is probably more commonly if haphazardly
used than any other. It is practised *immediately* before performing the
activity. You may be standing at your starting position or sitting nearby.
Lucinda Green, five times winner of the Badminton Horse Trials, locks
herself in the lavatory since this is the only place where she can rehearse
undisturbed. The rehearsal is short, compact and inclusive of all the major
components of the activity. An archer might take fifteen seconds, a high
jumper half a minute. If you are a gymnast about to perform a high bar
routine, the rehearsal might take as long as your routine. One British canoe
champion rehearses his slalom run immediately before the race. He times his
rehearsal and if it differs more than three seconds from his projected time, he
repeats the rehearsal until he has it right.

Instant preplay is like priming a pump. For a pump to draw water from
a well one must first pour a little water down its spout. Your body needs
similar attention. There must be a smooth transition from the pre-
performance activity of walking around, talking to friends, repairing
equipment and a dozen activities related or unrelated to your performance, to
the performance itself. *Instant preplay* provides such a transition.

Even if you have managed to set the non-related distractions aside you
may still be only 'thinking' about what you are going to do. Remember, your
nervous system is the co-ordinator of your movement. The body performs
according to the messages that you send. *Instant preplay* facilitates the shift
from abstract thinking to doing by initiating 'thought' in your body's
language: the language of seeing, feeling, hearing, smelling and tasting.

Instant preplay is used only for closed skills – skills which are repeated,
predictable and not affected by interaction with any other performers. Some
sports, such as snooker, archery, diving and golf are made up entirely of

closed skills. Others consist largely of open skills (their performance depending on interaction with team mates and opponents) but have a closed skill that can occur midway through the competition, such as a conversion kick in rugby or a penalty in soccer. Still others consist almost entirely of open skills but have skills which are 'half-closed', such as a short corner in hockey (which initiates a period of open skill competition) or a winning volley in tennis (which closes such a period). In rugby, the abrupt change from the open skills of running the length of the field and adapting to a variety of situations to being still enough to concentrate on converting a try can be difficult. A brief *instant preplay* helps to focus on the kick you have in mind.

In American football, the placekicker whose job it is to convert all the field goals as well as kicking the punts and kickoffs must suddenly make the transition from sitting on the bench for half an hour to appearing on the field in front of a huge crowd to produce the all-important three points. An *instant preplay* helps make that transition. In tennis, a brief *instant preplay* can help you produce your very best service when a point away from a crucial game, just as it can steady you when you are serving at thirty-forty and four-five down in the final set.

Dwight Stones, the American high-jumper and former world record holder, instant preplayed every jump. In his book *Golf My Way* (Simon and Schuster, 1974), Jack Nicklaus writes:

> *I never hit a shot, not even in practice, without having a very sharp, in-focus picture of it in my head. It's like a color movie. First I 'see' the ball where I want it to finish, nice and white and sitting up high on bright green grass. Then the scene quickly changes and I 'see' the ball going there: its path, trajectory and shape, even its behaviour on landing. Then there is sort of a fade-out, and the next scene shows me making the kind of swing that will turn the previous images into reality.*

Significantly, he adds:

> *Just make sure your movies show a perfect shot. We don't want any horror films of shots flying into sand or water or out of bounds.*

- *The exercise*
  - To carry out this exercise you may find it necessary to learn the *basic performance practice* technique first in the quietness of a room at home. In any case, it is advisable to perfect your *instant preplay* routine in training sessions before using it in competition.
  - The skill you are to perform and the time you have available before the performance will determine how long your *instant preplay* will last. It could be anything from five seconds to two or three minutes and it could involve practising the preplay just once or several times over. You will soon know what works best for you. You will also know where to practise it, whether at the start of your run in the long jump, standing before the parallel bars in gymnastics or behind the service line in volleyball.
  - You will probably be upright so take a deep breath and as you let it out allow the tension to drain to the floor for a moment, as if letting a

○ heavy overcoat slip from your shoulders. You may not need to close
○ your eyes but at that moment imagine the *feeling* of performing the
○ action you are to perform, at the correct speed and in all its complexity.
○ This visualisation is best done immediately from the 'inner viewpoint'.
○   If your sport involves a target, watch the bullet, the arrow, the dart
○ or the ball go precisely where you intend and, if this involves an arm
○ movement, make sure you follow through. Then take another deep
○ breath, open your eyes if you *did* close them, take stock again of your
○ surroundings and, without hesitation, perform the action you have just
○ visualised.

During performance or 'as if . . .'

This mental rehearsal differs from the other four in that, except in its
formulation, it doesn't involve withdrawal from your surroundings and
certainly doesn't involve closing your eyes. Instead it is akin to acting a part,
performing 'as if' you were someone or something else which represents a
quality that you want to emphasise in your performance.

    Mohammed Ali's poetry didn't win any awards but who can forget his
jingle: 'Dance like a butterfly, sting like a bee'? It personified his agile
movement around the ring and the sharp accuracy of his attack. Why does
'the Golden Bear' immediately conjure up the picture of Jack Nicklaus? Why
do American ice-hockey teams choose names such as Boston Bruins or the
University of Michigan Wolverines?

    Athletic nicknames, images and symbols evoke feelings which are hard
to express but which 'plug' the athlete into a quality of performance admired
by all sportspeople. Searching we might light on such words as 'grace', 'flair',
'fluidity', 'endurance', 'aggression', and 'consistency' but the reality is often
more complex.

    Dr Richard Suinn of Colorado State University used visual imagery
when training members of the U.S.A. Olympic Biathalon team. One of his
athletes once had difficulty making the transition from the strenuous cross-
country skiing to a stable position from which to shoot at the targets he met
along the course. With Dr Suinn's help, he was able to find an image which
represented the quality he wanted to evoke: it was the Rock of Gibraltar.
Thereafter, immediately before shooting, the athlete evoked the sense of
being the Rock of Gibraltar and momentarily acquired complete steadiness.

    Steadiness is essential for archery too. Many archers think they are
blown around and can't shoot when it's windy. One British archer we've
worked with deals with such conditions by shooting 'as if' she were a steel
stake in the ground.

    Tottenham striker Steve Archibald had a period when he felt he'd lost
something of his sharpness around the goal mouth. During a *top performance
practice*, in which he described to us what he was experiencing, he suddenly
said 'I feel like an elastic band, taut and ready to snap forwards.' Having
practised evoking this image off the field, he was able to use it later during
competition as he approached the penalty box.

    We've worked with a runner who acquires the fluidity of 'a babbling
brook', a sailor who regained his aggression when he remembered that, as a

child, he was like 'a snake that no-one could get near', a tennis player who realised during a mental rehearsal that when she plays confidently she is like 'a junior Margaret Thatcher' and a well-known golf professional who realised that *his* image of confidence was of a man in a pin-stripe suit going into a restaurant.

There are as many images and symbols as there are athletes. Some sound simplistic, many sound strange, but their use is widespread and effective. Sometimes we're still surprised. Another sailor, who is excellent at making up ground, but when in the lead was affected by the shouts of those behind him, announced one day that he'd won his race at the weekend by sailing as if he was Orpheus. Orpheus? 'Yes,' he said, 'it's a fairy tale. The way I get the beautiful woman is not to be tricked by others shouting to put me off. If I turn around I turn into stone.' (The fact that legend says Orpheus *did* turn round and *didn't* turn into stone made no difference!).

You may feel that you lack a particular quality altogether but probably you only fail to express it for one reason or another. The fact is, if you can recognise that quality in something or somebody else, and if you can find an image for that quality, that quality must already exist to some extent inside *you.* In psychological terms, you have been 'projecting' the quality on to the outside world and the '*as if* . . .' exercise is a way of rediscovering the feeling of that quality within yourself.

A less fanciful but as effective form of '*as if* . . .' visualisation is to use the image of another competitor in your sport who for you expresses the quality you seek.

- *The exercise*
  - Take some time to clarify the quality that you need to develop and decide whether it is a quality which should permeate your whole performance or one specific part of it only. You should also be aware whether this is a quality you have never had or whether it is one you have expressed in some past performance, if only for a moment.

    In the first case you should then think of someone who expresses this quality. Notice who comes to mind first and the precise action and situation that you see. Don't change it. For you the search for a symbol need go no further. For example, if the quality was aggression did you think of John McEnroe? What precisely was he doing as he flashed on the screen of your imagination? Close your eyes, relax and let the image become clearer, feel your way into the image by doing an *ideal model* rehearsal. What does it feel like to be John McEnroe? How do you move? Where is the tension and how is it released into the power and speed of your play? This feeling of aggression may itself suggest another image. You may complete the sentence 'I feel like . . .' by 'a tornado' or by 'John McEnroe.' Both are fine.

    In the second case, where you have experienced the quality before, close your eyes, relax and do a *top performance* rehearsal of one such particular moment. If you are with your coach describe what's happening out loud. Focus your attention on the kinaesthetic sense of performing this way and then eventually begin the sentence 'I feel like . . .' and see what happens.

In both cases, the next stage is to evoke a new scene, a picture of a competition in which you are soon to take part or of a recent competition that you remember well. See yourself in these surroundings performing some crucial action in a way that expresses the quality you have just experienced. Watch first from the outside and then move inside and again experience the feeling of playing this way – as a tornado, as John McEnroe or whatever – in these new surroundings.

You may want to practise this new rehearsal a few times during the succeeding week, but, as soon as you can, evoke the image at the start of a training session (begin by saying 'I feel like . . .') and then perform physically as if you *are* that image. Give yourself a set period of time to perform this way – perhaps five minutes initially – when your only objective is to be as exact an expression of your image as you possibly can. *This* is your '*as if* . . .' visualisation practice, the rest was a means of constructing it.

Once you have used the image confidently during a training session, it's available for you to use during a competition, whenever you need to draw on extra reserves, capitalise on a golden opportunity or hold your position at a crucial moment.

The following tips should help you perfect the exercise:

(i) The images should be generated by the individual who is using them. If your coach wants to help you use an '*as if* . . .' visualisation, he shouldn't approach you saying 'You're going to leap like a leopard.' or 'You're going to be as steady as the Matterhorn.' You may be terrified of big cats and may never have heard of the Matterhorn. Remember that the same image can evoke different responses in different individuals. A gazelle may evoke images of grace and agility for me and fragility and fear for you. Only when you find your own imagery will it be really effective. The right brain thinks associatively and the power of imagery lies in the personal associations it holds for us.

(ii) Don't confuse '*as if* . . .' imagery with *performance practice*. This type of imagery, if chosen correctly, carries some of the sensation associated with the quality that you want to evoke. Its use therefore is to stimulate that quality in your performance, not mentally to rehearse a skill.

(iii) Change symbols as necessary. After a while your image may lose some of its charge. You must then work with a new image, either for the same quality or for another quality that now seems more important. Images that have been discarded can sometimes become recharged and used again later on.

(iv) When you are working to evoke a quality in an isolated movement or specific skill, rather than in your performance as a whole, the symbol should be related to that movement. The Rock of Gibraltar may evoke stability for shooting but not consistency for a bowler in cricket. A bowler may identify with a catapult, a volleyball spiker with the image of a hammer striking a nail.

o
o
o
o
o
o
o

(v) Finally, remember that very often the image will not be primarily visual. '*As if*. . .' imagery often carries a large kinaesthetic component. As you do a *top performance* rehearsal become aware how your body responds and see if you can complete the sentence 'I feel like . . .' If you can, you have your image and it is that same feeling that you may expect to experience when you practise the visualisation.

Instant replay

The body has a very powerful sensory memory of its past performance. Some of us find it easier than others to tap this memory but the ability to do so can be cultivated. When leading mental rehearsal sessions at Tottenham, we were astonished to discover that almost every player could recall in detail the events of matches that were played months, if not the season, before. They may not have remembered the date of the match but, when describing some particular move of which they had been part, they knew with which foot they had received the ball, how many touches they took to control it, who was on their left and right, how far they ran with the ball and which foot, inside or outside, they used to pass or to shoot. It seems reasonable therefore to ask your body to remember an activity it has performed only minutes or seconds before.

Instant replay is the reverse of *instant preplay*. It is a visualised review of an action you have just performed, paying particular attention to the kinaesthetic sense. As with *instant preplay*, it is applied to the performance of closed skills and skills which are closed at one end: a dive, a vault or a putt can all be instantly reviewed; a tennis serve preceding a long rally can't, but a volley that died leaving your opponent sprawling under the net can.

Instant replay can be used to imprint a perfect action more deeply in your sensory memory. If you are a diver, *not* to instant replay your very first perfect forward one and a half somersaults with triple twists would be an exceptional chance missed. It can also be used to review a poor action and to assess what needs to be changed: thus *instant replay* forms the basis for the construction of a new *instant preplay*. The alteration of *instant preplay*, physical performance and *instant replay*, practised methodically and well, ensures fairly rapid improvement.

Although the kinaesthetic sense is of prime importance, you may have time to do one rehearsal from an outside vantage point. For instance, you could imagine you are your own coach watching from one side and making a critical assessment of your performance. This can produce unexpected insights into your technique. Rapid transition from kinaesthetic to visual imagery and back is not as difficult as you might think. Your imagination will seldom be unable to make the shift.

Make sure you feel at ease with the use of *instant replay* in training before you begin to use it to rehearse positive actions in competition. Using it to rehearse and adjust negative actions in competition requires more experience. You don't want to make any major changes in your techniques at that time but eventually you will be able to use *instant replay* to diagnose the minor adjustments that can and should be made.

- *The exercise*

Choose a time at a training session when you have just performed a particular skill and have time to replay it mentally. Stay where you are, whether standing, sitting or lying down. Take a deep breath, exhale and relax. Then re-create the scene of a moment earlier. What did it feel like to prepare and then to perform that skill? Imagine for a moment it's happening again now. How are you using your body? What parts of it move? How free or controlled is your movement? What quality were you expressing?

If you've time, go back to the beginning and become an observer. Notice if there is any part of your body which you had forgotten about. This can be important. If you want to replay the scene another time, go back inside and notice what you were thinking immediately before you performed the skill. What feelings did you have? Did they contribute or detract from your performance?

Is there some slight technical adjustment to make? If so, re-edit the memory, maintaining the positive qualities which you thought were of value and introducing the changes which will improve your perform-ance. Then replay this revised version. Later, when you need to perform this same closed skill again, use this new version as an *instant preplay*. As we said before, eventually you will be able to use the alternation of *instant preplay*, performance and *instant replay* during competition to good effect.

Performance review

We first developed this form of mental rehearsal with Mark Blencarne (who subsequently won the Archery Gold Medal at the 1982 Commonwealth Games). After a particularly good competition we decided to do a visual review of the performance instead of verbal analysis. As with the soccer players, we were struck by the extraordinary degree of detail that his memory retained. As he recounted his rehearsal, he discovered new information and insights. He realised that surrounding factors were as important to him as the details of his performance: what he felt like when he woke up that morning, how he dressed, the state of his equipment, who he was competing against and so on. As he ran through the rehearsal, we asked him the questions: 'What were the highlights of the day?', 'What were the most challenging moments?', 'What was your emotional state?', 'How was your concentration?' It seemed that, for him, the most meaningful and surprising elements of his recall were the less tangible ones – his attitudes, feelings and fine shades of perception during that day.

We discuss the importance of logical analysis following competition in chapter 5 but much valuable information about the event is reached more easily by a *performance review* visualisation. This is usually done some time after the event, at home or on the day of your next training session. If you can play the event over then without censoring your mistakes or exaggerating your strengths you will find it a surprising and enjoyable exercise. It can tell you more than a video for, in addition to the physical elements of your performance, you will re-experience the intangible subjective elements: the emotional and mental components. This technique can provide information either on your performance as a whole or on specific aspects – the warming-up, the fluctuation of arousal, the effect of your emotions, the pattern of your stamina or the moments of 'peak experience'. You can then use this information to prepare for the next performance. Ideally, you will come to perform such a review as a matter of course. As we shall see, it is a technique to be cultivated, for it can be used in a wide variety of circumstances.

- *The exercise*
  It is always best to ask your coach or instructor to be with you to take notes when you recount your rehearsal aloud and to ask you questions that help you retrieve still more information. If you can't use your coach, find a team mate and listen to each other in turn. If that is not possible, talk to a tape recorder and play it back later.

  Sit somewhere quiet, close your eyes and relax. Begin to re-create the day of the event: How do you feel as you wake up? How did you sleep? What are you having for breakfast? How do you feel – physically, emotionally and mentally?

  Remember yourself travelling to the competition. Are you on time? Notice the weather. Once you have arrived, see what strikes you about the place of performance, what things you like and what will be a challenge. Notice the spectators. How do you feel about them? Then consider your opponent or opponents and the people in your own 'team'. How do you feel about them? Now warm-up and then notice what you feel and your state of mind as the competition begins.

  Then let your memory range over the competition in whatever sequence it likes. What are the highlights of your performance? How do you feel about your team mates, your opponents and the officials? What is the best part of your performance? What is least good about your performance? What would you change? Do you start well? Do you finish well? Is your form consistent throughout? Notice how you feel at the end and what you do to warm-down.

  Then pause for a moment and take a deep breath, letting it out slowly. As you return to the beginning of the day and briefly review the whole event, let your attention settle on three aspects of your performance which you remember as being valuable, exceptional or somehow outstanding. Take a moment to note what characterised these aspects physically, emotionally and mentally. Then repeat the process and notice three things which you could do better or differently. Notice what characterised these aspects of your perform-ance, physically, emotionally and mentally. What can you do in the future to make your response more appropriate and achieve better results? The changes may be big or small. Allow your imagination to come up with some solutions.

  Having done this, go through the day one last time, without judgement or evaluation. When you have finished, open your eyes and write down the three valuable aspects of your performance and the three things you could have done better. Use this information as a guide to your training the following day.

28-29 SCISSORS (Big Solo)
80-81 X HOOK
24-25 D.S.O.
23 'Z' IN
76-77 DINO
T-78 'X' HOOK
P.361 'Y' SLANT
P.98 Dbl. GO

5
ANALYTICAL THINKING

Analytical 'left-brain' thinking complements visual 'right-brain' thinking and can also be used to improve your sports performance.

In this chapter we look at the techniques of determining long- and short-term goals, preparing for and reviewing a specific event, and the positive use of evocative language.

The two hemispheres of the brain

Research into the function of the brain has suggested that its two hemispheres organise distinct modes of thought and perception. Although this division may be less clear than first supposed, it provides athletes and coaches with a valuable outline of the different ways in which the mind affects sports performance.

It seems that we perceive time with the left hemisphere and space with the right. The detail or parts of an entity are perceived by the left, the whole with the right. The left perceives things taking place in sequence, the right perceives them simultaneously. The left hemisphere is the seat of our verbal skills, the right hemisphere of our visual skills. Logical and analytical thinking is accomplished with the left hemisphere, intuitive perception with the right. The left hemisphere also controls the right side of the body and the right field of vision, whereas the right hemisphere does the reverse.

These skills seem to complement one another. If we practise our verbal skills, our analytical thinking improves; or if we spend time learning to paint, we appear to develop our intuition.

It is clear from the table that our educational system has a heavy bias towards developing left-hemisphere abilities. These are the skills which are considered most likely to help a child to 'get on in the world'. Right-brain skills are considered to be of little practical use and, if taught at all, are only done so in the context of leisure activities. However, the same body of research shows that to function optimally a person needs to develop the skills of both sides of the brain. The professor who goes dancing, the accountant who paints, the writer who gardens and the artist who plays chess find renewed zest and inspiration when they return to their regular work.

Sam Wyche, offensive co-ordinator, San Francisco 49'ers — some analytical thinking in action.

Sport offers ample opportunity to develop, use and also to misuse both left- and right-brain skills. Visualisation in its various forms is a right-brain skill that can benefit sports performance. The use of a material or pictorial symbol to remind you of a physical attribute or quality of performance that you want to attain is another such right-brain skill. When Christopher Reeve took on the part of Superman he felt he 'looked like a piece of asparagus'. So he pinned a comic-book picture of his character on the wall and said, 'I've got to look like that and be as fit as that!' He started training and eventually achieved his goal. On the other hand, allowing your mind to dwell on and repeatedly play back a negative performance with no specific objective in view or to sit day-dreaming in a team tactics meeting are inappropriate, habitual *misuses* of your right brain. In this chapter, we will look at possible uses and misuses of left-brain analytical thinking.

Table 3:   Functioning of the brain

	LEFT BRAIN	RIGHT BRAIN
Functions:	Governs the right side of the body	Governs the left side of the body
	Governs the right field of vision	Governs the left field of vision
	Deals with input sequentially	Deals with input simultaneously
	Perceives the parts	Perceives the whole
	Perceives time	Perceives space
	The seat of verbal skills	The seat of visual skills
	Logical and analytical thinking	Intuitive and kinaesthetic perception
Positive techniques:	Goal-setting	Visualisation
	Planning and review	Symbols
	Formulating evocative language	
Negative habits:	Chattering mind	Day-dreaming in meetings
		Allowing mind to play over mistakes

When the left brain helps

You can always use clear analytical thinking effectively before and after sports performance. With 'closed' skills (repeatable actions that are not directly affected by the movement of another competitor, such as vaulting in gymnastics, diving in swimming, service in tennis, a penalty kick in rugby) you can use analytical thinking in a positive way before and sometimes after the specific action as well as before and after the performance as a whole.

However, the less time you have between thinking and doing or the more complex the activity that follows such an action, the less easy that will be.

Left-brain skills can be used to aid your performance in a variety of ways:

(i)   to set your long- and short-term goals
(ii) to plan and review your performance at a specific event
(iii) to formulate language that instils a positive attitude

Goal-setting

It is essential that you have clear long-term goals. Discussion between you and your coach or your coach and the team is the start of preparation for any competition. It is then that your objectives and the pattern of training is decided. This is just as true when planning a new season. If you are a tennis player, your season's objective might be to improve your volleying so that you can play confidently at the net, or as a cricket player you may wish to improve your fielding in the slips. However creative and intuitive you are, you should be clear early on what your goal is to be and how you will achieve it. For gifted players with a record of unpredictability and unevenness of performance, this process is particularly important. A player who relies on spontaneous flair alone has few inner resources to which he can turn on a bad day.

The following exercises should help you plan your training around achieving your long-term goals.

Deciding priorities

We sometimes find that an athlete can identify several long- and short-term goals but still seems to lack motivation. Most often this is the result of his having failed to decide his priorities. These must be worked out, either alone or with your coach, if you are to train consistently with a sense of enjoyment and self-motivation. The following exercise allows you to do this. It takes about forty-five minutes.

- *Part 1*
  You'll need four sheets of paper. On the top of the first sheet write LIFETIME GOALS and then take five minutes to write down as many such goals as you can – which competitions you want to win; what point scores or times you want to achieve; how you want to train, what kind of money you would like to make if you are a professional; how long you want to play; in which part of your sport you wish to excel, and so on. Aim at finding a dozen or more. Write down anything that comes into your head. Even if you sit and think only for two or three minutes, allow a full five minutes for ideas to come. Then stop, turn the paper over and don't look at it again.

  Now take the second sheet of paper and at the top write THREE-YEAR GOALS. Then again write down anything that comes to mind, without worrying about what you wrote on the previous sheet. After five minutes, stop, turn the page over and don't look at it again.

Take the third sheet of paper. At the top write THIS SEASON'S GOALS and write down all the goals you want to accomplish this season. It doesn't make any difference how important or how trivial, write them down. At the end of five minutes, stop, turn the paper over and don't look at it again.

Then take your fourth sheet of paper. At the top of it write ONE-MONTH GOALS and repeat the procedure.

Now return to the first sheet and read through your lifetime goals again. Take a couple of minutes to reflect which ones are really important to you, which ones are significant but not No. 1 priorities, and which ones are something you would like to do but which are not imperative. Choose the *three* goals which are most important to you and beside each one write 'A'. These are now your 'A' priorities. Then write 'B' beside three of the remaining goals, so that these are identified as your 'B' priorities – these goals are important and you would like to achieve them but they don't have the same urgency or central importance as the 'A' priorities. By all of the remaining goals put a 'C'. These may ultimately be something you want to accomplish at some point in future. There is, however, no urgency in putting them into action, but you may at some future date want to review their relative importance.

Now do the same thing with your three-year goals. Choose three 'A' priorities, three 'B' priorities and label the rest 'C'. Repeat the procedure with your season's and one-month goals.

Now sit back for a moment and reflect. How well are you working towards accomplishing your one-month goals? – your season's goals? – your lifetime goals? If you still feel you've identified your goals correctly, give yourself another twenty minutes to complete the second part of the exercise, as follows.

● *Part 2*

Look at your one-month goals. For each of your 'A' priorities, choose *three* things or 'action steps' which you will do in the coming week which will set you on the way to achieving those goals. They might be large or small steps, it makes no difference. For each of your 'B' priorities choose *one* thing you will do in the next week to accomplish these priorities. You need not make any commitments for your 'C' priorities at this time.

Now go back to your action steps (you should have nine for your 'A' priorities and three for your 'B' priorities). By each action step write a particular date within the next week by which time you will have put that step into action. For example, if one of your 'A' priorities is to reduce your tennis service faults by 20%, you may have chosen as one of your action steps to spend more time practising your second service in order to avoid double faults. So set a particular date and time where you will concentrate on practising your second service. Then make sure that you follow that commitment. Or perhaps your priority is to increase your stamina in the final 100 metres of the 1500 metre race.

Your action step may be to get a friend to pace you specifically for that part of your race. Set a date and place for telephoning him and arrange the practice. The more specific you make your action steps, the more you will commit yourself to fulfilling them.

Now turn to your season's goals. For each 'A' priority choose *one* action step you will take in the coming fortnight. Again choose a date by which time you will have taken that action step.

Then turn to your three-year goals. For each 'A' priority choose *one* action step which you will put into effect within the next *month*. Set a specific date by which you will have put that step into action.

You now have a number of action steps to be taken over the next month. If you find this process working for you, after a fortnight go back to your one-month goals and see which of your priorities you are meeting and which ones need further action steps. Perhaps some of your 'B' priorities have now become 'A' priorities or you have accomplished some of your 'A' priorities and so have room for another one. Choose one of your 'B' or 'C' priorities and upgrade it.

At the end of the month, give yourself a new set of one-month goals and choose 'A', 'B' and 'C' priorities for the new month. Decide the steps you will take towards realising the 'A' and 'B' priorities according to the procedure outlined above. Then choose further steps towards your season's goals and your three-year goals. Each month you can also choose one step to take towards a lifetime goal, making a commitment to put it into action within the succeeding four weeks.

In our experience, this is the best way of outlining a clear and consistent programme for training and performance in your sport. As you work with the system its effects become cumulative. As you reach the first of your goals, you begin to get a clearer picture of what you really want from your sport and how to accomplish it. Obviously the process can be applied to other areas of your life as well.

Intermediate goal-setting

The following exercise is designed to help you implement your long-term goals. Goals must be realistic but, even when they are, something more specific and tangible is often needed along the way to maintain your motivation. We developed this exercise when working with a soccer player who was recovering from a bad knee injury and was afraid of practising some particular ways of kicking the ball. Setting some intermediate goals along the way and working towards each in turn proved to be the answer. As with a number of such exercises, this should be done with your coach or sports psychologist.

• Take a piece of paper and then choose a specific goal you want to achieve (here we have the example of recovering confidence after a knee injury but the exercise can be used equally well to help you win a particular race or to perfect a particular skill). Now write down on the left-hand side of the page a list of all the hurdles that stand between you and your goal. The soccer player in question wrote down such things

	15 Aug		21 Aug		28 Aug	
Ball rolling away	10	1	10	1	9	3
Full toss	8	5	7	10	6	20
Ball at standstill	7	10	5	20	4	30
Ball from right	5	20	7	10	5	20
Ball on first bounce	5	25	4	30	1	unlimited
Ball from left	3	40	1	unlimited	1	unlimited
Ball rolling towards me	1	unlimited	1	unlimited	1	unlimited

as kicking the ball as it rolled towards him, as it rolled away from him, when it was still, when it came from the left, when it came from the right, when it came full toss, and so on. Having completed the list, go back and evaluate each hurdle on a scale of one to ten – one being something that would be very easy for you to do and ten being almost impossible.

Now reorganise the list so that ten is at the top, nine next and so on. Start a new column to the right of the list and write the date at the top. Then, next to each type of practice, write how difficult the task is out of ten and the number of repetitions you will do each time you train. In the case of the most difficult practice it might be once or even not at all. For the sixth-most difficult practice it might be between eight or twelve repetitions and for the least difficult task it might be anything from thirty to fifty times. Then do these repetitions in training.

Next week return to your list and start a new column to the right with the new date at its head. Now think about each task again and notice which seem less difficult now than before and whether any seem more so. Mark out of ten how difficult each task seems and then set up a revised number of repetitions for each skill, based on your experience of the previous week.

Bring the chart up-to-date on a weekly basis, until you have achieved your long-term goal.

Preparation and review

Generally speaking, you should use your right brain during performance to monitor your technique and your left brain before and afterwards to choose or assess your tactics. A valuable left-brain exercise is to plan and review each performance from the physical, mental and emotional point of view. Of course all sportspeople do some kind of preparation and review – most at least prepare physically and mentally – but few do it in a consciously structured way.

Preview/review exercise

This exercise uses left-brain thinking to assess how well you prepare and review a competition. When Scottish gymnastics coach Gordon Forster first introduced it to his national teams, he discovered that there were significant gaps in one or other of the three preview and three review categories. Some gymnasts did little emotional preview, others omitted physical review and the gaps and emphases had a significant link with the gymnasts' strengths and weaknesses.

● Draw up a chart like the one below, think back to your last major event and write down what you did to prepare physically, emotionally and mentally for that event. Then choose one thing that you've written down that you feel you did particularly well and write that down again before listing those things that you *didn't* do, which you now feel would have helped. (It's better to give yourself credit before criticising yourself.) Having done this, give yourself a score out of ten for your overall preparation and fill in the review column on the right in the same way.

EVENT:

DATE:

PREVIEW	REVIEW
How did you prepare	How did you review
(i) Physically?	(i) Physically?
(ii) Emotionally?	(ii) Emotionally?
(iii) Mentally?	(iii) Mentally?
What was your strongest point?	What was your strongest point?
What else could you have done?	What else could you have done?

In the following pages we consider physical, emotional and mental preparations and review and describe with examples, the factors which you might well take into account when preparing for and reviewing future events. Note that preparation includes the procedures outlined in chapter 1 but begin much earlier than the moment when you arrive at the place where the event is to be held.

Physical preview   A good athlete knows, respects and co-operates with his body. Gradually you build a routine of warm-up exercises which corresponds to your own needs. Your physical preparation for any specific event will probably include work on the technical skills you are most likely to use, deciding on diet and the times for eating and sleeping for the days prior to the event, choosing the way to travel, where to stay (and who with), the clothes to wear and ensuring that clothing and any equipment you need are as you prefer them to be.

Some time before the event you should take time to relax and tune in to any special needs that your body might have. Afterwards you do those physical warm-up exercises that seem most appropriate. Sometimes you may want to consult your doctor or ask your physiotherapist for a massage.

Each athlete, even athletes belonging to the same team, will have different physical needs. At White Hart Lane, whilst most players got messages from Mike Varney and some spent time reading the programme in the lavatory, Ray Clemence, garbed only in underpants, danced from foot to foot for ten to fifteen minutes, Ossie Ardiles had a mock boxing bout with trainer Johnny Wallace, Garth Crooks and Steve Perryman each did stretching routines in the changing room, whilst Graham Roberts, Tony Galvin and Paul Miller all went out to do some skills work on the pitch. At this stage there was no pressure at all for the players to conform.

Your coach can help you to discover your needs but ultimately this is something you have to do for yourself. This isn't always easy and can be particularly difficult when you are exposed to the tastes, patterns and rituals of other members of a team. You may need to be quiet and alone before you can hear your own body's 'voice'.

When the Scotland volleyball team did its physical warm-up prior to either a training session or a match, we would always allow ten minutes for individual stretching and skill work before asking the players to work in pairs. In the case of a training session, skill and tactical work would consist of exercises involving the entire team but players took time to tune into their own needs and then to one other player before working together as a group. (I'd often allow the same process at team meetings. Having asked a question, I would allow time for each player to be in touch with his personal response, then a moment to share this response with one other person and finally we'd have a full team discussion. – JS)

Learning to identify the correct physical warm-up procedure may be a matter of trial and error and for this a log or work journal is invaluable. In a team situation, your coach can monitor these journals and help you understand one another's needs. He can then gradually devise a systematic pattern of preparation for the team as a whole, which takes your differences into account.

Emotional preview   Emotional preparation means tuning in to your passing mood, as well as recognising, accepting and preparing for the needs which don't seem to change. It may be as varied as physical preparation and equally individual. A coach who insists that everyone goes to the cinema the night before a match is attempting to reinforce team spirit – but the attempt will fail because the genuine personal needs of some players are frustrated by the exercise.

Some athletes find they can best psyche themselves up alone; others prefer to be with a crowd or specifically with members of their own team, drawing on and contributing to the team spirit. Some need to begin the process several hours before the event, whilst others are more quickly aroused and must be careful not to peak too soon. Finding out what is right for yourself and ensuring that this is done is part of your left-brain process of preparation.

Physical relaxation is a technique that affects feelings as well as the body. A young tennis player, drawn against Martina Navratilova in the first round of the Wimbledon Championships and having to play her first-ever match on the Centre Court, may be understandably nervous. For her, it may be important that she relaxes only an hour before the start of play, thereby keeping her excitement within positive bounds. On the other hand, a top-seeded player in the same event, drawn to play against another unknown on an outside court may need to begin her emotional warm-up as soon as she gets up in the morning. For her to relax an hour before the match would be disastrous.

Nevertheless, each athlete needs to check into base level of relaxation at some time and begin the psyching-up process from there. Experience laid upon experience – whether match upon match, match upon argument or match upon a long-delayed family reunion – leads eventually to loss of performing edge and even to physical injury. In April 1982, when Tottenham was involved in the final stages of four competitions (the F.A. Cup, the League Cup, the European Cup-Winner's Cup and the League), the stress of playing three matches a week was intense. Many players were unable to relax fully between games and subsequently became injured. That month, no less than nine substitutes played in the home match against Liverpool.

Too many players in such teams lose touch with the quiet point within themselves. Just as there is a need for us to dream, so you need to begin your emotional warm-up from a point of letting-go or of inner calm. All that you have to determine is when the process should start.

Your emotional needs may be intuitive, illogical or even superstitious. Yet if you feel better-prepared when putting your shoes on before your shirt, who is to say you are wrong? The value of ritual is that it is associated with a specific mood which is re-created as the ritual is performed. It forms an observed part of many an athlete's preparation. Graham Roberts made sure that he was last to leave the Tottenham dressing room. The All Black New Zealand rugby team do their dance and chanting. Basketball teams stand in a circle with one hand inside, grasping the hands of the other players.

Under 'emotional preparation', you would also include some other practices described in chapter 1: tuning in to helpful aspects of the place and identifying and dealing with distractions, whether those of the place of competition or of feelings. This is best accomplished straight after a relaxation or on arrival. Over-anxiety can be controlled by techniques similar to the one described for distractions and a fuller discussion of this is given in chapter 6. Such visual techniques are, of course, right-brain, but planning in advance where and when to use them is a function of analytical thinking.

Emotional preview can use the rational left hemisphere of the brain to ensure positive feelings during a competition. One of the most famous examples of all has to be that of Arthur Ashe's preparation for the Wimbledon Final of 1975, when he beat Jimmy Connors. Borg and McEnroe had yet to emerge, and Connors, reigning champion at 22, seemed likely to hold the title for several years. Ashe was given little chance but he had prepared for this match down to the last detail – physically, emotionally and mentally. He described this in a recent interview, finishing with an account of the final game when he served for the match at 5–4. 'I'd planned this too,' he said, 'how I'd serve the last game if I got there. It's the tensest moment in any match and you're less anxious if you know what you're going to do.'

Mental preview   The third type of preparation is mental preparation. Your objectives, what you want to achieve or get out of a particular event, and how you intend to succeed in this should be decided (and preferably written down) some days in advance.

Athletes competing in individual events, such as cycling, shooting, swimming and track and field, in which the result is decided by time or score, often have very clear long and short range targets and also the incentive to keep a record of their progress throughout the season. With team sports, we often find that no such targets have been set and that the objective of the team as a unit is confused with the objective of the individual player within that unit. In fact, the team decision on objective and tactics is only the starting point for your mental preparation. You must then decide how you can best deploy your talents to help the team reach its goal.

When we first went to Tottenham, we found that although the manager and coach would comment on the performance of individuals and occasionally devote a training session to 'individual coaching', when we asked a player what his objective was for the coming match he would reply 'To win.' If we asked, 'Fine, so *how* are you going to win?' he'd say, 'We're going to concentrate on defence for the first twenty minutes and "earn the right to play".' We would then say, 'Okay, so now how are *you* going to do this?' and at last he would begin to think and then to explain how he was going to do this in terms of his own position on the park.

Your preparation will also be coloured by previously determined personal *long-term* goals, ways in which you are working to improve over the course of the season as a whole. You may for instance have been working on your interaction with another player, both during training sessions and matches, to the point where you're ready to try out some particular combination. Your mental preparation would therefore include making a secondary objective to put this combination into practice should the moment arrive.

Ideally, decisions on both long- and short-term objectives are made in the course of personal talks with your coach, who will then monitor your progress, but if necessary you must do this alone and ask some other member of the club to watch and assess how far you fulfil these objectives during the competition.

It is important to think creatively about your objective. Ask yourself the questions: 'How do you feel about your game?', 'What are you aiming to improve this season?', 'Given the team's tactics for the coming match, how are you going to pursue those aims yourself?' and so on. If, as a forward in a hockey team, you identify the need to be sharper in attack, ask yourself *how*, *how often* and *when* you intend to be sharper. This might lead you to the clear decision that you will take the ball into the penalty circle at least five times in the first half – something that you would be able to check.

Sometimes though, particularly in 'open skill' team games, the coach must draw up complex analysis sheets if he is to have enough reliable information for a mental review of an athlete's performance. When Keith Burkinshaw was coach at Newcastle United, he used to have an assistant who drew lines on a sheet of paper to represent the ground covered by a specific player. It was Josef Kozak, the Czech coach to the Italian men's volleyball team in the 60s, who taught me to 'score' each player on each of his service receptions, according to how accurately it was delivered to the setter.

Service Reception			
	Good	Fair	Bad
Steve D	//	ЦН //	///
Fred	/	ЦН /	/
Steve T	/	ЦН	ЦН
Alan	ЦН /	//	/
John	///	ЦН	///
Peter	ЦН	ЦН ЦН	/
Ian	/	//	/
Dave		/	/

The more precise your objectives, the more instructive your analysis can be afterwards. If your only objective is to win you will finish the competition with relatively little gained, even if you succeed. Should you fail badly, you will be unable to use your analytical left brain to take the edge off your disappointment and if your opponent is so weak that you win easily you will come away with little sense of achievement.

Like the Tottenham players, you must go beyond identifying your desire to win and decide *how* you're going to win. Furthermore, your objective has to be realistic. If a victory seems unlikely, it becomes imperative that you set yourself a secondary target of improving some aspect of your performance.

Several years ago, the Scottish men's volleyball team (with the author, John Syer, as coach) played in the European Championships for the first and only time. When the draw was made, we discovered that we were to play world champions Czechoslovakia in the first match. I realised then that to go into a match with no specific objective was to ask the team to win and to risk a harsh blow to morale should the result be particularly bad. Those players who doubt their ability to achieve the unstated objective (to win) are a drag on the team from the start, whilst those who go into the match with misplaced confidence experience the severest reaction to defeat.

In the event, I called a team meeting to discuss what we could best gain from the opportunity of playing Czechoslovakia in the first match. At the end of a thoughtful discussion, at which it was recognised that Czechoslovakia would have to serve accurately at least 45 times before they could win (three sets of 15 points won on service) we decided to work on our service reception. Accordingly, I focused our training sessions on this skill and then set up an elaborate analysis sheet to record each player's performance at service reception during the match.

The match was indeed lost – 15/1, 15/3, 15/1. The Czechoslovakian attack tore over, round and through our defence, but the game had an excitement all of its own that gradually aroused the small Italian crowd. So intent was our service reception that we were able to mount some sort of attack and actually won service many times. The game lasted all of 40 minutes, instead of the half hour we had expected. Afterwards in the changing room, instead of the dejection of defeat, players crowded round to see the analysis sheet, looking to see whose reception had been best. The next day, through fine service reception and against all expectations, we came close to beating Turkey.

If victory seems certain, then you must set your targets higher and attempt something technically that you haven't yet achieved. Such planning will help your concentration because it brings challenge and enjoyment into a competition that might otherwise be a disagreeable experience for winner and loser alike.

Review   Like the preview, a full account of physical, emotional and mental review may cover things done over the period of a few days after the event. Any activity which helps you return to a balanced state of being, anything which 'ties up loose ends', should be counted a part of the review. Whereas your physical and emotional preparation should follow your mental preparation, your physical and emotional review should precede your mental review.

Physical review   Physical review includes warming-down exercises, taking a shower, relaxation, sleep, eating, drinking and receiving treatment for injury. Cleaning, checking and repairing your equipment also comes into this category.

After any type of sport it is essential to let your body warm-down slowly. If you are the first in the bar you are probably not allowing sufficient time for your body to recuperate thoroughly after its exertions – and hence are more likely to suffer injury.

Steve Perryman is the longest serving player in the Tottenham side. As first team captain, he represents the players at innumerable meetings as well as assuming responsibility on the field. Despite these additional demands and the intensely physical nature of his game, he is hardly ever injured, and, during the 1981/82 season, was the only Tottenham player to play in all sixty-five first team matches.

No doubt the usual explanations for his durability – toughness, determination and a sense of responsibility to the club – all hold some part of the truth but it is more significant that he is nearly always the last person to get in and out of the bath and to dress after a match or even after a training session.

Steve Perryman, Captain of Tottenham Hotspur Football Club – first out on the pitch, last out of the bath.

Emotional review   Emotional review includes anything that allows you to digest the feelings aroused by the event, whether you're feeling angry, elated, disappointed, frustrated or excited. Since eating and drinking are social events they too count as emotional review if they allow you to release the tension of your feelings. Going to the pub with other members of the team is a time-honoured ritual with many team sports, a chance to talk out and re-live the experience at one remove.

In fact, the range of possible activities that allow you to calm your feelings is infinite. The person on one of our courses who, when asked what he did after a particular tennis match, replied, 'Burnt my racquet.' had got the idea and was pointing out that not all solutions are peaceable. Some people do allow the frustration and anger generated by a disappointing event to explode into other situations, shouting or bursting into tears at the slightest provocation – although to be fair the same people would probably be equally expressive of their excitement and joy.

Others find that dancing, singing, cooking, watching television or gardening serve the purpose just as well. For many the game is forgotten as soon as they return to family life, whereas some disappear on a long walk alone. The important thing is for you to notice your post-match behaviour over a period of time and become aware of what helps you most in the face of success and of failure.

One day we were exploring Chris Hughton's inability to relax. As he talked, he suddenly realised that his habit of going to the supporters' club after each home match and discussing the game endlessly with his friends was one that he wanted to change. Contrary to the needs of many team players, Chris's were to be alone with his wife and family. He'd been going to the supporter's club because that was where he'd arranged to meet his wife but once there he hadn't liked to take the initiative to leave. Going home was the form of emotional review that was right for him. Making the change allowed him to release a long-held residual tension.

Emotional review begins immediately after a match. At Tottenham, Keith Burkinshaw and Peter Shreeve did much to assist the process, walking around, sometimes sitting beside players encouraging them to speak.

This is the time for your coach to ask the vague question: 'What do you think of the match?', meaning: 'What do you *feel* about it?'. Such a question would be a vague and lifeless way to start a Monday morning analytical discussion because by then the emotion is spent but, as a way to help you release your immediate feeling, it is ideal. No-one is looking for a reasoned response at this stage, not even the manager. That can be left until Monday morning.

Mental review   Finally, mental review is the process of looking back and judging to what extent you attained the objectives you set before the event. If they were all reached, should you have aimed higher? If it was a good performance, what factors still require improvement? And if it was a disaster, what one aspect might nonetheless be grudgingly termed a success? There are lessons to be learned from any performance so that, however good or bad, it leads to another step forward.

Feelings immediately after the competition are often strong. It is then hard to be objective and notice either the imperfections in a good performance or the perfections in a bad one. The time for your mental review is after you have completed your physical and emotional review – very often two days later, the Monday morning or evening following a Saturday afternoon event. Clear discussion and assessment with your coach and fellow athletes is then possible but because the emotional involvement has decreased it might also require an effort to reconsider the event at all. If you have a coach he must gauge the timing of this review carefully and be imaginative in his use of the discussion techniques that we describe in chapter 8.

A professional team that meets to train on a Monday morning begins with a mental review of the previous Saturday's match. The coach starts by asking 'What were our objectives?' and then 'How far did we achieve them?' Usually some specific theme will then emerge from the discussion, which becomes the basis for technical or tactical training for the rest of the week.

The clearer your original objectives, the easier it will be to assess whether they were attained. It is important that you should first express your subjective opinion but eventually analysis sheets or the objective view of a friend will provide incontrovertible evidence and, used sparingly, can be an effective way of facilitating change.

You can learn lessons from any performance and should review victories as thoroughly as you do defeats. It is important though that you ask yourself what you did well, before deciding what needs to be improved.

Mental review leads you naturally into your preview of the next occasion. Having completed the review of the competition, you can set new objectives in relation to the lessons which you have learned.

The coach's preview and review   We have already suggested that your coach should monitor the preparation and review journals of his athletes. He has two other tasks: to work out his own process of preparation and review – how *he* prepares for and recovers from an event in which he is involved as coach. Whether his coaching performance is good, mediocre or bad will partly depend on this. If he is a team coach, he should also devise preparation and review schemes for the team as a whole. Obviously, team training on days prior to the competition and team warm-up on the day, constitute physical preparations. He may also have to take decisions on travel, eating and sleeping times.

The emotional preparation of athletes will be anything which he does to raise morale or team spirit. He will usually do this at the meeting immediately before the match. The team's mental preparation will also be accomplished at meetings and will be the process of arriving at team goals and tactics – decisions which you then have to take into account when considering how to move towards your long-term objectives during the coming competition.

The team's physical review would more often be the job of an administrator than your coach and would include ensuring that there are hot showers, food and comfortable transportation home.

Emotional and mental review would mostly be accomplished at team meetings, after you and your fellow athletes have done your personal reviews at home. If morale or team spirit has become fractured in the course of defeat, you should all be encouraged to identify and explore the resentments you feel towards team mates or coach. Disgruntled athletes who voice their dissatisfaction privately to certain team mates or to people outside the team are an undisclosed drain on team spirit. Exploring such sentiments in a team meeting needs care. However, when carried out effectively, it not only plugs the leak but, by bringing strongly felt disagreements and grievances to light, can lead to new perceptions and a stronger team spirit than before.

In our experience, overwhelming victory can sometimes be as disruptive to team spirit as catastrophic defeat, perhaps because team spirit is only aroused in response to a challenge. When an objective is attained, new goals need to be set. Otherwise the team may fracture again into a group of self-satisfied individuals. We look at this topic further in chapter 8.

The team's mental review will be an assessment of performance in relation to the goals that were set and the way in which it was decided they should be achieved. Your coach's first question at a review meeting should be: 'Who will remind us what our goals were for this competition?' and the second: 'How far do you feel we achieved them?' – the same questions that you should already have asked yourself in relation to your personal objectives.

Formulating evocative language

One other way in which analytical thinking can help performance is in the formulation of evocative language to help create a positive attitude. There are at least three types of evocative language.

Affirmations

A sentence which gives you a positive attitude and which you repeat or read at intervals for some days prior to a competition is called an affirmation. Probably the most famous affirmation in sporting history is Mohammed Ali's: 'I am the greatest!' Not only did he believe it but so did millions of spectators around the world.

The most effective affirmations are those which occur spontaneously in your own speech. When discussing a past performance, you may identify some aspects of it which you want to regain, emphasise or perfect. Your sports psychologist, coach or fellow athletes must listen for such expressions, draw your attention to them and help you to reformulate them into positive statements. When Chris Hughton said, 'I need to talk more and take more responsibility for my side of the field,' we changed it to: 'I talk and take responsibility for my side of the field.' David Hemery was very impressed when he heard heart-surgeon Dr Christian Barnard say, 'Man can achieve anything within the scope of his imagination.' Instinctively he turned this to spur his training. In effect he made an *affirmation* of his own: 'I can achieve anything within the scope of my imagination.'

Some *affirmations* are doubly effective because of their vivid language. In fact, if you listen carefully, you'll find that athletes who use vivid metaphors are the norm rather than the exception. Key experiences are often expressed in this way, especially when you are relaxed, with your eyes closed and describing a mental rehearsal. Whoever leads the rehearsal for you should make sure to have a pen and paper ready. Often a question which prompts you to describe how you *feel* as you perform the visualised action will bring a particularly striking reply.

Steve Archibald, the Tottenham striker, once came to a session saying that he felt he had lost the edge of his ball control. Later, as he visualised a moment in a past game when he had had this control, he suddenly said 'I feel like the Lord of the Manor.' When the session was over, we reminded him of the sentence and during the following week he used it as an adjunct to the mental rehearsal practice – a quick way back to his feeling of being in control.

Once you have your new sentence, write it down in your own handwriting or print it carefully on to a card. Then stick it somewhere so that you see it and unconsciously rehearse it throughout the week before your next competition. Each time you repeat the sentence, you reinforce the emotional feeling that, for you, accompanies the action it describes.

Evocative words

Choosing a single word which evokes a particular quality in an athlete's or a team's performance is the left-brain equivalent of using a symbol. As with an *affirmation*, it is essential that the word first arises naturally in the athlete's speech or a team discussion.

When Tottenham were discussing the defence of their F.A. Cup championship against West Bromwich Albion in 1983, the Manager asked the players to reflect on the quality that had characterised their performances in Cup matches over the previous two successful seasons. Over and again the word 'battling' was used and it cropped up in training sessions throughout the week. On the following Saturday, his pre-match talk emphasised this one evocative word. Meantime his assistant, Peter Shreeve sensed that the Cup itself *symbolised* the quality of 'battling' and brought it from its cabinet to the changing room. The players responded by raising their game from a string of poor League performances to winning form.

When boxer Marvin Hagler was training for his successful defence of the middleweight World Championship title against Tony Sibson, he described the way he begins to build up to a fight: 'First give me a name. This time it was 'Sibson', so I went to work right away. He's in my head all the time. When I'm running, when I'm training, he's all I see.' For Hagler, the name 'Sibson' became an *evocative word*.

On one of our courses, Llanelli rugby coach, John Maclean, told us he used to stand on the touchlines shouting 'Push!' at his scrum, to no effect. When he began to shout 'Drive!' instead, the response astonished him. He also now uses the word 'ruck' when talking tactics at team meetings; 'Before, I used to say "loose scrum" and that's exactly what I got.' 'Drive' and 'ruck' are *evocative words*.

Slogans

Many athletes and coaches have instinctively known the truth of the dictum 'energy follows thought'. Eddie Fuchs drummed the same tactical message,

'Pressure him!' into both Joe Frazier and Ken Norton as he trained them for their victories over Mohammed Ali.

Bill Nicholson, the former Tottenham Manager who led Spurs to the League and Cup double in 1961, calls such messages *slogans*. These were formulas which he repeated so often that they forever ran through his players' minds. Some of his most well-known *slogans* were: 'Play the way you're facing!', 'The man without the ball makes the play.', 'Engage. Disengage.', 'One ball back, the next goes forward.' and 'Make the ball do the work.'

When the left brain hinders

Analytical thought devoted to preparation for or assessment of performance is always positive but when you begin to analyse your performance in mid-stream there is trouble.

Timothy Gallwey, in his books on the 'Inner game', describes this process in detail. He personifies analytical thought that occurs during performance as 'Self 1', the voice that reminds you when you play tennis that you must relax, must follow through, must win this point, must play well because your father is watching, and invariably provokes nervous tension and interrupts the flow. Flow is the characteristic of 'Self 2', a 'Self' without words that when undisturbed is quite aware of what to do and how to do it. If Self 1 is a left-brain animal, Self 2 is his intuitive right-brain counterpart.

Having drawn attention to these two different identities, Gallwey points out that Self 1 is *so* judgemental that he can be distracted by even the simplest task. If asked, he will happily spend long stretches of time working out how high the ball is as it crosses the net or exactly when the ball hits the ground or is struck by the racquet, thereby leaving Self 2 to play his fluent intuitive game. Gallwey will therefore ask his students to call out their estimate of the height of the ball above the net as it crosses from side to side, or he will ask them to shout out 'Bounce!' each time the ball bounces and 'Hit!' each time it is hit. When your Self 1 is so engaged, Self 2 has a chance to show what a fluent player he really is.

For your coach, of course, it is different. He will use his analytical left-brain during your performance. However, Gallwey is careful to point out that if he notices you making some recurrent technical fault – not following through, playing the ball when standing too square to the net or with your weight too far back – he should not then give this information directly to you. If he does, he will be giving your Self 1 more ammunition and during the next rally Self 1 will be shouting 'Follow through! Follow through!' and Self 2's fluidity will quite disappear.

When Self 1 observes without judgement, Self 2 is unhampered, so your coach might well ask you to notice *how far* you follow through on each stroke – without saying how far is precisely right. The tendency then is for you to become aware of the sensation of following through and, in so doing, to make any necessary adjustments intuitively. Kinaesthetic sense is closely linked with intuitive right-brain thinking and the process of visualisation that we discussed in chapter 4.

6
DEALING WITH ANXIETY

Emotions can inspire or inhibit your performance. Positive emotions can often fire you to attain your peak but when your excitement turns to anxiety or your aggression to anger, you will probably begin to make mistakes.

If anxiety heightens beyond a point of positive arousal, there are ways to lower it again to an acceptable level. In this chapter we show how to convert what has become an alarming situation or a frightening ordeal back into an exciting challenge.

Anxiety and tension

It's probably the athlete's experience and expression of feelings such as determination, delight and team spirit that ensures sport its spectator following. Certainly you won't reach your potential until your performance becomes a vehicle for emotional as well as physical and mental creativity. Physical and mental strength and skill achieve little if the emotional counterpart isn't there to provide the driving force. However, sometimes emotion or an excess of emotion will inhibit your performance and, of all such occurrences, the incidence of anxiety is the most common.

Sportspeople are affected by varying degrees of anxiety. In fact, we have already identified anxiety as a necessary component of arousal and it's sometimes difficult to distinguish it from excitement. However, there is a point on the ascending scale where you reach a degree of over-arousal and, from here, anxiety will affect your performance adversely. Many athletes hover on the edge of over-arousal and usually their own experience teaches them how to regulate the emotion.

Much further up the scale is the intense anxiety that accompanies memory of a past traumatic event. These may be memories of an injury or of losing an important competition in a particularly agonising way. As a volley-ball spiker, I (John Syer) once played on a court where the posts were supported by small metal extensions fixed to the floor. Half-way through the match I landed, after spiking the ball, with my left foot on the extension. I tore the

Overleaf: A skier on the Sierra Nevada, California. How does one overcome the fear and anxiety associated with steep and dangerous slopes?

muscles of my ankle and leg so badly that I was in plaster for three weeks. Much later, with my leg completely healed, I found that whenever I received a set that was high and near to the post (the perfect set for a No. 4 spiker) my run-up lost pace and my jump lost height so that I was unable to take advantage of the situation. Somewhere at the back of my mind was the memory of the accident.

One Gloucestershire golf professional came to us at a time when he was incapable of hitting a good drive into the sun. A year previously he'd been leading in the last round of an important competition, had teed-up, driven down the fairway and lost sight of the ball. The same thing happened twice more, he returned a ten for the hole and missed all the medals. The memory stayed with him so that he became tense and anxious whenever he subsequently found the sun shining straight down the fairway.

All anxiety is accompanied by physical tension. When anxiety heightens beyond the point of positive arousal, the accompanying tension may be termed neurotic. Sometimes the tension comes from being stuck between the fight and flight response, part of you wanting to be there and part not. Anxiety stimulates your flight response, but this is blocked by your wish to compete. This means you are using one set of responses to restrain another set and the result is like treading on the accelerator and the brake at the same time.

Often this deadlock is accompanied by a fixed heightened awareness of one's surroundings. Anxiety is in many ways, particularly in its physical manifestations, very like anger where, for a moment at least a block of tension is experienced and the angry person not only sees red but colours visibly too. The interesting thing is that when the tension is released the alertness and clarity of perception can sometimes remain, so that a sportsman having this experience may suddenly find himself having a 'peak experience', where everything flows and he seems to know a split second in advance what will happen next.

Reducing anxiety

It is just one more characteristic of our bodymind that anxiety cannot coexist with relaxation: when physical tension is lost, emotional and mental tension are released. We have suggested that the quickest way of relaxing is first to identify the tension and then to slow down and deepen your breathing. When you are feeling over-anxious, the first step is to ask, '*Where* am I anxious?' and notice which parts of your body are tense.

Recognition (in the case of the cause of anxiety) is the first step towards creating change. Turning your attention to your physical sensations will already distance you a little from your feelings. In a broader perspective, recognising in advance which situations are likely to be anxiety-producing will allow you to plan and practise methods of dealing with these situations, which can then be put into effect instantaneously. It may also help you to either avoid or exploit such situations in the future.

Having found the points of tension, you can alter your breathing, relaxing from the head downwards (if you're sitting or standing), spending additional time 'watching' and releasing the muscles that are particularly tense. Once you're relaxed and still alert, you can use a variety of visualisation techniques to gain a more enduring control.

There are in fact a variety of ways you can deal with anxiety, all of which involve lessening physical tension but some of which are left-brain rather than visualisation techniques. For the sake of simplicity, let's consider techniques that can be used in three different situations:

(i) where you are over-anxious prior to a competition

(ii) where you are over-anxious during a competition

(iii) where you find yourself having to face a situation which evokes memories of some past traumatic event

Prior to competition

You may already have your own preferred way of lowering your arousal level when anxious before a competition. In a team sport, this needs some careful handling by your coach for whom things would obviously be easier if all the squad could prepare effectively in the same way. Some of you will prefer being on your own, others want to interact with the group. Some will find exaggerating their feelings, acting them out, making fun of them, will release the tension, others will deepen and slow down their breathing.

Here is a list of other related techniques.

- 1 *Mental rehearsal of skills or movement*
  This is preceded by relaxation and will be a programme that you have set up and practised regularly before, involving skills which you'll use early in the competition.

- 2 *Positive self imagery*
  Again preceded by relaxation, this is a mental rehearsal of yourself incarnating a specific positive quality whilst performing various actions. These mental rehearsals should be short and interspersed with further moments of slow breathing. (See Chapter 4, 'As if . . .' visualisation.)

- 3 *Affirmations*
  Here you review meaningful sentences which you have recited to yourself during the build-up to the day of competition. Each sentence affirms some positive strength or quality of your performance. You can alternate the affirmations with visual imagery of the same qualities.

- 4 *Simple physical skill practice with evaluation*
  You can perform this alone watched and evaluated by your coach or with a partner with whom you will interact during the event. If with a partner, an additional benefit will be the strengthening of a sense of team spirit between the two of you. The skills that you practise should be ones which you perform easily and well. Physical movement in itself often releases tension and anxiety.

5 *Segmenting goals*

I (John Syer) went on a skiing holiday for the first time in ten years and frequently found myself stuck half-way up the mountain facing an impossibly steep and icy slope, strewn with enormous moguls. I would stand at the top, petrified, until my instructor noticed me and I'd find that time and again he'd make illuminating suggestions. On one such occasion, I told him I was afraid and he asked, 'On the scale of one to ten, *how* afraid are you?' Without pause for breath, I replied 'Ten out of ten.' 'Right,' he said, 'but you're looking down to the bottom of the slope. How afraid are you of going from here to that mogul over there?' and he pointed at a mound not too far away. 'Well . . .' I said, 'perhaps four out of ten.' 'Can you deal with four out of ten?' my instructor asked. 'Yes.' I said. 'Well, let's go.' he replied.

Fritz Perls defines anxiety as the gap between the now and the future. Frequently we find that the things of which we are afraid loom somewhere in the misty distance. Focusing on the first thing which you have to do and realising that that at least is something you are reasonably able to perform, is often enough to get you started. Thereafter, things might be far better than expected. If they aren't, it is as well to check whether you are again 'looking all the way down to the bottom of the slope'; usually there is a 'mogul' not too far away that you can be reasonably sure of reaching safely.

6 *Changing fear into excitement*

Since the physical manifestations of excitement are similar to those of fear, it is worth at least trying out the statement: 'I am excited by this dive, this vault, this climb, etc.' just for size. If the fear is not a useful up-to-date emotion and not too highly pitched above excitement on the arousal scale, the silent affirmation 'I am excited' may be enough to evoke that feeling.

7 *Changing anxiety into energy*

On one occasion, when we were working with Barbara Lynch, she was preparing to shoot against the World Champion Susan Natrose. She realised that she felt powerless and negative as well as extremely anxious whenever competing against this particular shooter – and that not only did she always lose but that she always shot way below her potential. Discussion led to the understanding that she was investing Susan Natrose with all the strong qualities that she usually believed herself to possess. Barbara was then able to construct a visualisation practice which she called 'turning fear into energy'. In this, she saw Susan Natrose full of strength and energy in the form of light and then saw and felt this light flowing out of Susan into herself as she reclaimed the qualities she had 'given away'. Susan shrank in size and Barbara felt her energy and strength renewed. In the event, Susan still won but Barbara did better than she had ever done against her before.

8 *Catastrophic expectations*

Sometimes it helps to get a broader context to your anxiety, a mental equivalent to taking a deep breath and breaking free of the closed-in tension of your body. Considering how to reply to the question: 'What is the worst thing that could happen to me now?' has often led nervous athletes to explode their nervousness away in laughter.

- 9 *Creative distraction*
  This again involves retreating somewhat from the situation. The ideal distraction is one that involves helping your coach (or some other team member if it is a team sport) with a physical task.

- 10 *Other methods*
  If your team coach were to ask the team what methods you use to counteract over-arousal, he could well be surprised by the variety of response. At *Sporting Bodymind* courses we seem to have heard everything from taking a slug of whisky to putting on extra socks and stamping on the ground (in order to overcome 'cold feet'!)

During competition

You can use many of the above techniques during competition as well as before the event – especially in the case of closed skill sports, such as golf, diving, gymnastics and athletic track events, where there are rest periods between each burst of action. Two of the following additional techniques (the *black box* and the *quiet place* visualisations) need much practice before you can use them in open skill events, where there are few, if any, pauses in play – but the others work well with either closed or open skills.

- 1 *The black box*
  We described this technique as one to be used when warming-up. However, it was originally developed to deal with worrying distractions that occurred during competition. Not only does it help you to calm down but it allows you to review the distractions afterwards and work out how to turn them to your advantage, should they occur again.

- 2 *The quiet place*
  Following the early examples of Arthur Ashe and Billy-Jean King, many tennis players will close their eyes and withdraw for a moment from the tension of a close match, when changing ends. (See p. 51) For this to be effective you must not just 'leave' the match but actually 'arrive' somewhere else – an imagined place where you are alone and relaxed.
  When learning the *quiet place* technique, you need to find somewhere that you can sit undisturbed for five minutes, close your eyes, take a couple of deep breaths letting them out slowly and allow yourself to relax from the head downwards, feeling your body sink more heavily on to the chair as you do so. Initially your coach or a fellow athlete should lead the visualisation for you.
  After completing your relaxation, allow a moment or two of silence. Then visualise yourself alone in a place that is peaceful and where there

is no likelihood of your being disturbed. It may be indoors or out but most likely in a field by a river, a place in the mountains, somewhere deep in a forest or by the sea. If more than one place comes to mind, be aware which came to mind first and allow the other impressions to fade.

Notice what clothes you are wearing and what position you are in . . . If you are lying down, sit up and then let yourself relax in that position, noticing what is straight ahead of you – the objects, the colours, the line of the horizon and any faint movement there might be in the distance . . . Then look down at the ground . . . What colour is the ground? What sort of ground is it? Reach out and touch the ground and feel if it is rough or smooth, warm or cool, damp or dry . . . and rub your fingers harder on the ground before lifting them to your nose and seeing if it has a smell.

Let your hand drop and turn to the left. What do you see on your left? What objects? What colours? Notice the play of light and shadow and, as you look, be aware of the season, the time of day and of the weather . . . What signs of the weather can you see or hear, what signs can you feel on the skin of your face? The warmth of sunshine? The breath of a wind? The dampness of mist?

Then turn and look to the right . . . and again notice what you see on your right, what shapes and colours . . . and as you look to the right, become aware of the sounds that belong to this place . . . the hum of insects, the calling of birds, the sound of running water, of wind in the trees, or of children calling in the distance . . .

Then look behind you . . . look above you . . . and settle back into your original position, looking straight ahead, seeing again the line of the horizon, the shapes, the colours and any faint movement there may be there in the distance . . . Let yourself be aware of how it *feels* to be in this place, this place where you can completely relax, notice all that is peaceful around you . . . Allow yourself to stay there a little longer. . . .

Now let the scene fade for a moment and without opening your eyes become aware again of your body on the chair in this room. Become particularly aware of your hands . . . Now take the thumb of your left hand in the fingers of the right and squeeze your thumb with a gentle pressure . . . and, as you feel this pressure, let yourself drift back to your *quiet place* . . .

See yourself there, notice the clothes that you are wearing if you are wearing clothes, and the position you are in. If you are lying down, sit up and then let yourself *be* in that position, looking out at the horizon if you are out of doors, noticing what is straight ahead of you, the objects, the colours, the line of the horizon and any faint movement there might be in the distance . . .

The process is then continued as before . . . and when you have looked all around again, settle back into your original position, gazing straight ahead . . . and eventually decide to come back to the room, let go of your thumb as you do so, before opening your eyes.

Holding your thumb as you go into the visualised *quiet place* can be developed with practice into a 'trigger' technique, helping you eventually to feel yourself instantly in that restful situation. It may take a little time for the connection to be learned and you may find that you can return easily to your visualisation without using the trigger. However, eventually the technique will allow you to reach your *quiet place* instantly, for just the moment that you need it: during a break in your sports performance. The trigger can be especially useful in a tense situation, where you realise that your anxiety or arousal level has gone far too high.

3 *'As if . . .' visualisations*

There were many times during the first part of my recent skiing holiday, when my fear level was 'ten out of ten' as I stood at the top of some precipitous icy slope. Once, as I was standing there, two small boys noisily slithered helter-skelter past and almost straight down, elbows and ski sticks and skis all over the place, shouting to each other as they disappeared rapidly out of sight.

Involuntarily, I burst into laughter. 'What are you laughing at?' asked the instructor, quick as a flash. 'Those two boys, they are so funny, so carefree!' I replied. 'Don't you remember what it is like to be a child?' he said . . . and he made me pause a moment, imagine the feeling and then take off pretending to be those children to the best of my ability. I loosened up, I *felt* carefree . . . and, when I eventually fell, I was laughing again.

Another time the instructor made me look at a route down the mountainside and asked me to imagine an animal going down there easily, smoothly and fast. 'What animal did you see?' he asked. 'A fish,' I said. 'Right, imagine how it feels to be a fish and let your skiing show me as I watch you go down.' And I skied down as if I were a fish.

4 *Focusing on a movement pattern*

The 'as if I were a fish' visualisation not only helped me develop the qualities of ease and grace in my skiing but incidentally distracted me from my fear by focusing my attention on my kinaesthetic sensations. You can accomplish this switch without visualisation by focusing your attention on any part of your physical movement, particularly some aspect which you have been trying to improve in training sessions.

5 *Building a routine of task-oriented patterns*

During your performance you will most often find your thoughts following one of two major patterns: 'task-oriented' or 'self-oriented'. Task-oriented patterns of thought are those which focus on the physical task immediately at hand: following through on your tennis swing, keeping your weight on your uphill ski, keeping your weight forward in your volleyball dig etc. Self-oriented patterns focus on thoughts with more subjective content: evaluating how well you are performing, wondering what your coach is thinking, anticipating accepting the medal or cup at the end of the competition.

Building a routine of task-oriented patterns of thought helps you to focus on the necessary physical skills and can be particularly useful

o   when you find yourself distracted by worries outside your immediate
o   control.
o
•   6 *Visualising music*
o   Barbara Lynch tells a story about Susan Natrose, who, it transpires,
o   has a strong religious background, and will steady herself before and
o   during competition by singing hymns beneath her breath. These
o   hymns have a strong rhythm and prevent Susan from speeding up
o   through anxiety or tension creeping in. Variations of this technique are
o   used by swimmers and skiers. As with any 'problem-solving' visualis-
o   ation, it is important for you to find your own images (in this case that
o   you select your own tune) for the emotive content of a specific image
o   will vary from person to person.

When faced with a traumatic memory

All mental training techniques, like their physical counterparts, require programmed practice if they are to be effective. It is in fact this concept rather than most of the techniques themselves which is most difficult for many athletes to understand.

In the case of techniques designed to deal with anxiety arising from a particularly unpleasant memory, more than usual care in their application and dedication in their practice are needed. Actually this borders on an area where the responsibility for such a programme should be that of a clinical psychologist, rather than the sports psychologist or coach, although the clinical psychologist would not normally be involved in problems arising from situations such as my volleyball injury or the golfer's drive into the sun.

Both the visualisation techniques described below begin with the assumption that the unpleasant or traumatic memory is indeed a memory and not a complete blank. Research done at the University of Iowa by D. H. Schuster at the P.A.M.F.A. (Psychological Assistance to Medical First Aid) unit showed that patients being treated for burns were frequently unable to remember the accident that caused them and that this memory gap blocked the healing process. The patients would therefore participate in therapeutic counselling sessions designed to lead them gently back to the time of the injury and to refocus their attention on the injured part of their body which they had avoided because of the original pain.

It was found that unconscious fear of pain can actually reduce circulation in an injured area of the body, maintaining tension and stress and reducing the elimination of toxins. When the patients retrieve their memory of the accident, the healing process takes its normal course. (It seems that the healing process may actually be speeded up when the patient is able to gain a visual image for that process and practises the visualisation regularly. Visualisation of a specific healing process such as increased activity of white blood cells or reduction of blood pressure can produce a measurable response.)

The following exercises are best led by a sports psychologist or coach.

1 *Progressive desensitisation*

The key element of this technique, described by Denise McCluggage in her book *The Centred Skier* (Vermont Crossroads Press, 1977) is the alternation of visualisation and relaxation. You are asked to think of seven or eight situations which arouse anxiety and which are related to the traumatic event. You should then list these situations according to how nerve-racking they are, so that at the top of the list is a situation which gives you just a frisson of anxiety – perhaps a level of four out of ten – and at the bottom is a ten-out-of-ten situation, similar to that of the original event.

My list for dealing with the volleyball accident might look like this:

4/10	Hearing that the match is to be played in the same hall as the one where I was injured
5/10	Someone saying 'Did you know, they still haven't put in socketed posts?'
6/10	Arriving at the hall to find some metal brackets holding the posts to the floor
7/10	A player in the opposing team saying 'I see you've recovered ....another player was injured last week in the same way,
8/10	Watching players start a spiking practice and seeing one stumble on a bracket as he came down
9/10	Receiving a set which seems to be drifting right out to the post whilst taking part in a spiking warm-up
10/10	Receiving such a set in the game, going for it, and realising there's no way I can avoid the bracket as I come down

Having made such a list, you then work with your coach or sports psychologist regularly over a long period of time, taking the 4/10 situation first. You'll be led into a relaxation and then asked to visualise the 4/10 situation. After describing it in detail, you'll be asked to transfer your attention to your body, notice where anxiety has made it tense, and go through the relaxation procedure again. Once you're fully relaxed again, you repeat the visualisation and continue to alternate relaxation and visualisation until the visualisation no longer causes you anxiety or tension. At this stage (probably at a subsequent session), you will deal with the 5/10 situation in the same way. Eventually, memory of the actual traumatic event will no longer cause you anxiety or influence your performance.

2 *Visual re-editing*

This technique was evolved from anthropological studies made of the

Senoi Indians. It was observed that when a child had a recurrent nightmare, the parents would ask him to first recount the nightmare to them and then to go back to the beginning, tell the same story but find a way to change the ending into a happy one. If, for instance, the child had dreamed he was being chased by a man with a knife, he might change it to realising the knife was really a message.

The child is then asked to tell the new version of his dream each night before sleeping. It is as if a new channel is being dug that eventually gets deeper than the old one and, at this point, the child wakes to find that his old nightmare has changed into a new dream.

The *visual re-editing* process is similar. You sit quietly, close your eyes and relax. You then play through the original traumatic event visually, describing it out loud to your sports psychologist or coach. You describe the scene in as much detail as you can, the colours, objects, people, movement that you can see, the sounds that you can hear, the weather that you can feel, see and hear. Having related the whole event, you then relax once more and consider what it is in the story that you have told which you felt then or feel now you might have done differently which would have changed the outcome in a positive way.

You then run through the new version of the event to yourself, setting the same scene as carefully and as vividly as before and marrying the new ending neatly to the same start to the story. Having run through it once to yourself, you can tell the new story, eyes still closed and talking in the present tense, to your coach or sports psychologist. If the story is not vivid, your coach should ask one or two questions, also in the present tense, to deepen this new experience. You then practise this new version for perhaps five minutes each day, alternating each run through with a thirty-second relaxation.

Some athletes we have worked with initially had scruples about 'changing the event' and 'kidding themselves'. We then made it clear that visual re-editing does not change either the event *or* one's memory of it. The crux of this exercise is that it changes the negative associations you have with the event and thereby eventually changes your response when you find yourself confronted with a similar situation.

3 *Intermediate goal-setting*
One analytical thinking technique for dealing with traumatic memories is intermediate goal-setting. We outline this in chapter 5. The example we give there is that of a footballer recovering confidence after a severe injury to his knee.

4 *Other techniques*
When athletes consult us on an individual basis to work with them on any such traumatic memory, we sometimes offer to introduce some simple gestalt and psychosynthesis exercises which involve role-playing and visualisation techniques other than those already described.

7
ATTITUDES AND CHANGE

How can you erase the image of yourself as someone who always tightens up at the critical moment? If you fade when confronted with an opponent you have never beaten, even though you regularly beat other players who in turn beat him, what do you do? If your team has a reputation for crumbling as soon as the game becomes more physical, how do you change your response? If you lose your form when it rains, can you do anything about it? How do you cope with a team mate who constantly irritates you?

These problems are similar in that they are all caused by your way of observing, interpreting and reacting to a particular situation. Solving such problems involves a change of attitude. In this chapter we present some exercises which will help you to escape from attitudes which limit your performance and to cultivate others which will bring improvement.

Attitudes

Attitudes are habits of mind. As with repeated movements which become second nature, we form patterns of thought and feeling about situations and events which eventually take on a life of their own.

Of course we need attitudes, just as we need learned patterns of movement to perform physical skills consistently. From the time we are born and begin to interact with our environment, we make decisions about what is happening in our world. Each second, we receive a welter of information from our environment and of this we have to make sense. When we see an object coming towards us, we must determine whether it is an aeroplane, a bird or a cricket ball. As babies we can't do this, but as we grow we learn to differentiate. A child can tell the difference between a rugby ball, a soccer ball and a volleyball. A football player can differentiate between six different soccer balls and tell whether a ball is spinning to the left or to the right as it comes towards him. The more intensely we concentrate, the finer and more subtle the distinctions we can make about the object of our concentration.

England Rugby Union XV – a daunting proposition.

However, we also tend to make distinctions between situations which are not so evident. Just as we decide whether a tennis stroke will be a drop shot or have top spin, we begin to prejudge our opponents according to our experience and according to the previous decisions we have made about that experience. This can lead to trouble.

Suppose you are a spiker at the start of a volleyball match, looking through the net. You see that the player opposite you is six inches taller, with long arms and legs. He looks strong and powerful and the other two front-line players look the same. Past experience tells you that when you play opposite such opponents their strength and size enables them to block you, so you decide to play cautiously, to dump over the block or to place rather than power your spikes. You may tighten up, lose height, hit into the block and become discouraged.

After twenty minutes your team is 8/13 down in the first set. Your coach calls his second time-out and addresses you directly. 'What's the matter with you?' he thunders, 'You're not attacking.' 'But look at the size of that front line!' you reply, 'I'm trying to place the ball.' But your coach has seen more clearly. 'Don't just look at their size. Watch how they play. The No. 2 player is tall but normally your jump is eight inches higher than his. And watch that central blocker. He's big, yes, but he's incredibly slow. There's often a yard between them when the ball is set to the end of the net.' And suddenly it strikes you that perhaps your coach is right and your instinctive tactical decision was based upon your response to their strength and height but ignored their lack of speed and agility. You go back on court and begin to change your attack but it's too late and you lose the set 12/15.

Obviously, the attitude you have about opposing strength and height is one based on previous experience. It serves its purpose and is a good starting point. The problem arises when you begin to let attitudes take charge rather than guide you: when attitudes become fixed or 'the truth' instead of a first step towards judging a situation. One of the strengths of any good player is his ability to learn from an experience and not have to be constantly relearning basic skills and strategies. But a second, equally important strength is flexibility: the ability to adapt to a new or unusual situation which may be different from or contradict his normal expectation.

We suggest that your attitudes be decisions about your experience, not set patterns. John Hilton became European table tennis champion largely because he was able to disguise the different surfaces on his bat and prevent his opponents from distinguishing the kind of spin he put on the ball. They were unable to adapt and he used their predictable learned responses to his advantage.

Let's be clear. We all have and need to have attitudes about ourselves, other people and the environment. There is no time, especially in the heat of competition, to work out all the possible interpretations of the signals that bombard our attention. We rely on our experience. No, our concern is to suggest ways of evaluating and changing counter-productive attitudes about recurring situations. You can alter your idea that you are a slow starter or that you crumble under pressure. You can change the attitude that you can't deal with opponents who have a physical advantage, that you are shattered by defeat or that you can't beat opponents who have a certain style of play.

These are counter-productive attitudes about your ability which can be replaced by productive ones.

Steps in creating change

There are five steps towards creating change, which apply when learning skills, when recovering from an injury, when improving concentration etc. We outline them here because the process is central to transforming unproductive attitudes. A new response can be created to old problems when the problems are approached with the right attitude.

- 1 *Recognition*
  Before you try to change anything of substance in your performance, you must first recognise what it is that you are *actually* doing. Nine times out of ten, having discovered what you are doing, you will be able to see what you are doing *wrong*. Only then can you choose the strategy which will bring change with a minimum of effort. Why scrap your cricket cover drive completely if some minor adjustment only needs to be made?

- 2 *Acceptance*
  Recognition should be accompanied by acceptance and you should accept what you are doing before you create change. This is one of our basic premises. If you have been acting in a certain way, whether it be shouting at the referee or twitching during your putting stroke, there was originally some underlying legitimate reason. Your current behaviour is based on a natural response to the situation that existed at the time that behaviour was learned. (See our section on learning in chapter 2.) You don't make mistakes or develop bad habits for no reason at all. Accept the fact that there is a good discoverable reason for your current state and that you are capable of making a change.

  Accepting your bad habit gives you an increased awareness of its underlying cause. Often it is a need which is not being met – more fitness training of a certain muscle group, a less distracting environment, more coaching in a skill, more patience with yourself, or more time to prepare a shot. By appreciating the unmet need and finding some way of meeting it, you can usually solve the problem or at least eliminate a major obstacle to creating change. A little judicious self-observation and reflection is often all that is required.

  It is our experience that when you give yourself a little understanding and acceptance rather than the constant criticism and browbeating to which many of us subject ourselves, you uncover an increased willingness on the part of all those uncontrollable and unconscious parts of yourself to co-operate with the process of change. Put simply, if you meet these needs rather than deny them, the parts of yourself which possess these needs are then more willing to join forces with you and your conscious motivation, rather than sabotage or resist the changes you want to make.

■ 3 *Co-ordination*

Co-ordination is the core of the changing process and the second half of this chapter will examine the techniques involved in more depth. Once you have recognised the problem and accepted the reasons for it, you are in a position to make a fairly specific decision about what to keep and what to change. Many of the *Sporting Bodymind* techniques discussed in this book may be used in this step and the next. Recognition and acceptance will have enabled you to list the different factors needing your attention. This third step involves plotting a course for dealing with them. You experiment with more spin on your forehand drive, with placement of your weight when driving, with the length of time you take to draw the bow in archery. On the mental level you rehearse certain skills more than others, you discover the right level of relaxation to precede a match, you decide whether you need to focus your concentration more on internal or external objects, or you use analytical thinking to evaluate your performance and set goals. At the attitudinal level you use '*as if . . .*' *visualisations, evocative words, affirmations* and other techniques covered in the latter half of this chapter to change your attitudes towards yourself, towards your opponents and towards the environment in which you perform. You weed out the non-productive habits and either begin to transform them or to substitute new patterns.

■ 4 *Integration*

Once you have identified a different, more appropriate response to what was previously a problematic situation you move beyond experimentation to the stage where you integrate the new response into the rest of your performance. You achieve this by consciously choosing the new response to the old situation whenever it occurs. The element of conscious awareness makes all the difference. You have replaced what was formerly an uncharted and uncontrolled part of your sporting self with a more conscious participation. Using *Sporting Bodymind* techniques, you can anchor this new awareness in physical, emotional and mental experiences.

■ 5 *Synthesis*

The final stage, synthesis, is the experience of the new pattern meshing perfectly with the rest of your approach and skills. Some new quality or potential then emerges and you find yourself playing in a way which goes beyond your past limitations. At its height this experience is as described by Pele, when he says he felt:

> *a strange calmness I hadn't experienced in any other games. It was a type of euphoria; I felt I could run all day without tiring, that I could dribble through any of their team or all of them, that I could almost pass through them physically. I felt I could not be hurt. It was a very strange feeling and one I had not felt before. Perhaps it was merely confidence but I have felt confident many times without that strange feeling of invincibility.* (Pele with Robert Fish, *My Life and the Beautiful Game*, Doubleday, 1977, p. 141.)

Bobby Jones describes a similar experience:

> *Of all the times that I have struggled around the golf course there are a few easy rounds that stand out in my memory. One thing stands out about all of these rounds: I had precisely the same feel on each occasion: I was conscious of swinging the clubs easily and yet without interruption . . . I had to make no special effort to do anything.* (Robert Tyre Jones Jr. *Bobby Jones on Golf*, Doubleday, 1966, p. 184.)

Peak experiences involve little or no conscious control. They are effortless. The five-stage process of changing counter-productive attitudes involves moving from recognition of the old to effortless performance of the new. Our experience suggests that when you begin to recognise the patterns of your personality, connections and associations are built which, over a period of time, add up to some kind of critical mass. The critical mass of awareness creates the base which allows a synthesis to take place. From this synthesis a peak experience or peak performance can result.

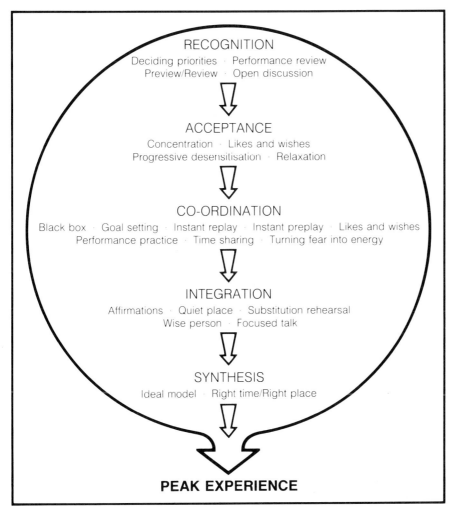

RECOGNITION
Deciding priorities · Performance review
Preview/Review · Open discussion

ACCEPTANCE
Concentration · Likes and wishes
Progressive desensitisation · Relaxation

CO-ORDINATION
Black box · Goal setting · Instant replay · Instant preplay · Likes and wishes
Performance practice · Time sharing · Turning fear into energy

INTEGRATION
Affirmations · Quiet place · Substitution rehearsal
Wise person · Focused talk

SYNTHESIS
Ideal model · Right time/Right place

PEAK EXPERIENCE

But enough of theory. How do you actually change negative attitudes or a counter-productive self-image? We have broken down the areas where you may encounter attitudinal problems into three categories:

(i) attitudes about yourself
(ii) attitudes about other people
(iii) attitudes about the situation in which you find yourself

Let us consider each in turn.

Self attitudes

Some of the most deep-seated and stubborn attitudes are the ones we create about ourselves. If ever there were self-fulling prophecies they are the ones which run: 'I can never drive properly when the pressure is on.', 'I've always taken a long time to get warmed up.', 'My backhand has always been weak.', 'I'm good for two sets and then my concentration goes.', 'I never really did have it in me to make the first team.' There are as many variations on these themes as there are athletes. A positive self-image is one of the most important and yet vulnerable assets you can possess. In the competitive situation where it seems there is always someone rumoured to be better, younger or more hungry then yourself, your positive self-image needs all the support it can muster from your attitudes and experience.

There is nothing wrong with the Mohammed Ali affirmation 'I am the greatest!' – if it has a realistic basis. But cultivating an appropriate self-image involves more than this. Your self-image reflects the sum total of your experience, thoughts and emotions. It is something which deserves considerable attention and gentle development. When we work with athletes on an individual basis, we usually spend considerable time helping them to explore their current attitudes before working towards any change.

The following exercises are all straightforward. Use them to discover what your self-image is as well as to cultivate the qualities you need to bring that self-image into balance. Take some time to recognise how you see yourself now. This will help you make appropriate decisions for where and how you need to implement change.

- 1 *The Esalen word game*
  This is a game inspired by a stay at the Esalen Institute in California. Find a place where you can sit alone for a few moments. Then choose some aspect of your sporting performance towards which you know your mental attitude could be improved. Then, with this aspect and a number of different examples in mind, write down and complete the following sentences:

  'It's difficult for me to . . .'
  'I hope that . . .'
  'If I . . . then . . .'
  'I'm going to try to . . .'
  'I can't . . .'

  When you have done this, take a moment to consider what you have written. Notice how the sentences reflect your attitude about the situation. Then rewrite the sentences, amending the first few words as follows:

'I'ts difficult for me to . . .' → 'It's a challenge for me to . . .'

'I hope that . . .' → 'I trust that . . .'

'If I . . . then . . .' → 'When I . . . then . . .'

'I'm going to try to . . .' → 'I'm going to . . .'

'I can't . . .' → 'I won't . . .'

Notice which of the changes make you feel more positive, as if the second version releases new energy into the situation you describe and suggests a new way of looking at it. Resolve to make these changes when you speak about your performance in future, making a conscious effort to interrupt and correct your own negative language.

2 *Affirmations*

We describe the use of *affirmations* in chapter 5. A somewhat different kind of affirmation can be obtained by another method in order to counteract a negative self-image. When you encounter an attitude which is difficult to change or a self-doubt which crops up regularly, stop and take a moment to verbalise what it is that you are actually thinking. Express it in as simple a sentence as possible. Then work out the opposite of that sentence, elaborate it a little and you have a personal positive valid affirmation. In effect, you are changing a negative statement for one that affirms that an opposite quality is already beginning to emerge. Here are some examples:

'I can't follow through on my backhand.' → 'My backhand is smooth and continuous and I follow through completely each time I hit the ball.'

'I always lose concentration on the sixteenth hole.' → 'As I approach the sixteenth hole my concentration becomes stronger and stronger.'

'I can't play well against Joe Bloggs.' → 'When I play Joe Bloggs, I find myself playing better and better as the match progresses.'

And so on. Make sure that your affirmation is always a positive statement. Don't change 'My backhand drive is weak.' to 'My backhand drive isn't weak.' For some reason that doesn't work. Say 'My backhand is strong and consistent.'

As you practise your *affirmations* you'll find that they begin to drive a wedge between your old self-image and the new one you are cultivating. They work even better when reinforced by a right-brain technique, such as mental rehearsal. Find an image that is the visual equivalent of your *affirmation* and practise the visualisation and the *affirmation* alternately. If you say the *affirmation* out loud so much the better. Repeat it to your mirror image whilst you shave or comb your hair. Try saying it under your breath whilst competing, especially when you find yourself under pressure. You might even find yourself turning your *affirmation* into a Mohammed Ali-type jingle.

3 *Evocative word cards*

Often, as you recognise the need to change an attitude, you find there is a particular quality which is conspicuous by its absence, one which you have never had or one which you have lost and need to regain. As we said in chapter 5, conscious repetition of the name of the quality can be used to evoke it. Writing the word down on a card, as you might do with an *affirmation*, will speed up the process.

Let's say that, as a golfer, your approach shots have become very erratic. Reflect a moment and let a word come to mind which embodies the quality you seek. Don't rush the process. Consult your kinaesthetic sense as well as your intellect. When the word that describes that sense comes clearly, hang on to it. Then carefully write it down on a card – say the word is 'consistency' – and then see how you can make the card more expressive of your sense of consistency, perhaps using coloured pencils or pens. You may also want to write the word 'fairways' or 'irons' somewhere, just to make it more specific.

Now place the card in a strategic place: on your bathroom mirror, on your desk at work, inside your locker door, as a marker in a book you are reading, in your diary or anywhere else where it will catch your attention several times a day.

From then on the card will do its work by itself, particularly if you have spent some time making it. Leave it for a week or two until it no longer seems to have an effect or until some other problem has surfaced which needs attention.

4 *'As if . . .' visualisation*

When a change of attitude involves developing a particular quality such as persistence, grace or quick-thinking, you may also use the *'as if . . .'* visualisation described in the chapters 4 and 6. Close your eyes and allow yourself to relax. After a while, let the quality come to mind first as a word and then as an image. The image that represents this quality may be of a particular person (for instance, Bjorn Borg for consistency), of an animal (maybe a tiger for ease and power in a volleyball spike), or an abstract symbol (such as a tree for sturdiness, a rock for stability or a bulldozer for power in a rugby scrum). Whatever your image, stay with the first one that comes. Don't try for something more exotic. The one that comes spontaneously will be the most meaningful. Use it!

Watch this image or symbol and notice how it expresses the quality you want. Don't let your analytical mind tell you that the image is silly. Spend some time with it. After a while, try imagining that you *are* that image, that you can feel what it is like to *be* that image. Then, take that feeling with you as you go back to an event where you needed the quality that the image represents and play one part of the event through in your mind, feeling yourself expressing the quality in your performance. Practise this new mental rehearsal for two or three minutes, then return to the room and open your eyes but bring the feeling of the quality you were expressing back with you.

If you take time to practise this rehearsal regularly, you will find it possible to evoke the new response during competition, experiencing the quality of the image and letting it flow into your performance. Drawing a picture of the image, taking time over it and then placing it

o strategically as you did with your *evocative word card* will reinforce the
o mental rehearsal.
o
• 5 *Exploring polarities*
o One of the problems in changing a negative attitude is that we take
o ourselves too seriously. A way out of this is to exaggerate. If things are
o bad, make out they're worse, if they are terrible, pretend they are a
o disaster. Then take a step back and look at yourself. What do you
o recognise? How much truth is there here and how far does the
o exaggeration show that you were indulging in a distortion of the real
o situation all along?
o   We have a game called *failure and success* that involves finding a
o partner and taking two minutes to tell him what a failure you are. Spare
o no detail. Elaborate all the ways that failure manifests itself in your
o game. Imagine and explain your physical and emotional feelings when
o you play badly. What are your very gloomiest thoughts? After two
o minutes, you stop and your partner takes his turn. He has two minutes
o to convince you he's more of a failure than you.
o   Then you both take a deep breath, let it out slowly and get in touch
o with a feeling of supreme success. Then take your two minutes
o convincing your partner of the total change, noticing how you speak,
o how you move, what you feel and what you think. At the end of two
o minutes your partner has his turn.
o   If you experience the extremes of each pattern of behaviour
o you may notice later when you over-identify with one or the other
o and be able to prise yourself loose from a fit of emotional excess
o during a competition. This same game can be played with a
o number of polarities: controlling/without control, inspired/dull,
o quick/methodical, extrovert/introvert, etc.

Attitudes about others

How you think about yourself in relationship to your opponent makes a great
difference to the kind of game you play. John, a friend of ours, remembers a
summer of tennis in Scotland where he played regularly against two friends,
Daniel and Ed. John always beat Daniel and Ed always beat John. One day,
near the end of the summer, Daniel said to John over lunch, 'Oh, by the way,
I beat Ed yesterday.' 'You did what?' exclaimed John. 'I beat Ed,' Daniel
repeated. 'But how could you beat Ed? Ed always beats me and I always beat
you,' said John. Daniel gave John a run-down on his tactics and strategy but
had no set explanation. This exchange forced John to alter his attitudes. The
next time he played Ed he produced his best tennis of the summer and
managed to win.
    The point of this story is that there is energy blocked behind
inappropriate or out-of-date attitudes which is released back into your
performance when the attitude is shaken or changed. Sometimes our
performance is inhibited by an attitude that was never appropriate. Have you
ever been changing for a match when one of your team mates walked by

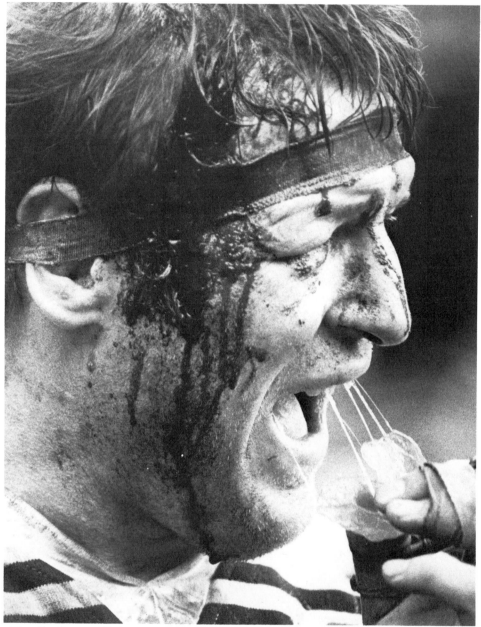

Charlie Stone, Hull Rugby League Club. 'I see . . . you have blood pouring down your face; I imagine . . . you wouldn't hesitate to run me down; and this makes me feel . . . very worried to say the least!'

without a greeting or a response? You find yourself disconcerted or annoyed, or you imagine that the casual suggestion that you made to him the previous day must have upset him.

During the ensuing match your communication is restrained and you pass the ball to each other less than usual. After the match, in the changing room, you finally take the plunge and ask him, 'Why aren't you talking to me?' 'What?' he replies. 'You didn't say hello when you came in today. And then you didn't pass the ball to me the whole match,' you say. 'What are you talking about?' he asks. Then you explain, 'I thought you were angry because I made that suggestion about our tactics yesterday.' Recognition dawns. 'Look,' he says, 'you've got it all wrong. I'm not angry about yesterday at all. I've just broken up with my girlfriend and don't much feel like talking to *anyone*.' As an afterthought he may add, 'I thought *you* weren't passing the ball to me because you didn't approve of my play.'

Attitudes about others are easier to recognise than self attitudes. Often they are easier to shift as well because we are not so attached to them. One of the problems with attitudes about oneself is that they become so familiar and comfortable that we don't recognise that they are counter-productive, even when it is pointed out to us.

The following exercise shows one way in which you can begin to recognise counter-productive attitudes you may have developed about *others*. There are two elements in the formation of attitudes. The first is previous experience in a similar situation and the second is the decisions made about that experience. This exercise also shows the way in which we make decisions about what we experience.

- 1 *I see . . . I imagine . . . and that makes me feel . . .*

  Practise this with your coach or a fellow athlete. Take a moment to look at him and say one thing that you notice. For example: 'I see that you have brought two racquets today.' He then says something he notices about you: 'I see that you are wearing new shoes.'

  The next part begins 'I imagine . . .' You state the first thing you imagine about what you see: 'I see that you have brought two racquets today and I imagine that you expect to break a string.' or 'I see that you are wearing new shoes and I imagine you have been playing well lately.' (The logic may sometimes only be apparent to the speaker!)

  The sequence must end with a response which begins '. . . and that makes me feel . . .' For example: 'I see that you have brought two tennis racquets, I imagine that you are afraid of breaking a string and that makes me feel wary of your service.', or 'I see that you have new shoes, I imagine that you have been playing well lately and that makes me feel less secure in my own game.'

  Notice that in both cases what you feel is based upon what you imagine, not on what you see. In other words you observe something about your opponent and your past experience combined with the attitudes you have formed about similar situations govern your response. This response may or may not be appropriate but it definitely isn't based on objective analysis of the here and now. So when some aspect of your opponent worries you, work out why. Obviously we don't mean you should dismiss all of your past experience. The majority of your attitudes may well be valid. On the other hand, it is worth finding out what percentage of your evaluation is hard fact, what is an educated guess and what is speculation. The sooner you can confirm suspicions and eliminate fantasies, the sooner you will adopt the right way to play your opponent.

2 *Analysis*

If you realise you have an attitude about a future opponent but can't think on what it is based, try to watch that person perform and make a systematic analysis of the skills in question. Coaches of First Division football clubs 'scout' other teams they are about to play. They gather together as much objective information as possible before making a decision on tactics. Out-of-date attitudes and unfounded assumptions can lead to a false sense of security or needless tension.

3 *'Transforming' your opponent*

Do you have a bogey opponent – someone who, for no obvious reason, defeats you every time and against whom you always turn in a below par performance? Although you can't change the opponent or play beyond your ability, you *can* change your experience of the situation and reshape your response.

During a period when the former English épée champion, Steven Paul, was having problems with continental opponents, I discovered that he held certain of these fencers in awe because of their impeccable style. In fact, they weren't necessarily better than him, for what Steven lacked in technique he could have made up in flair and aggression. Instead, he found himself retreating defensively. Since his whole performance is based on flair, attack and surprise, he inevitably lost confidence. This exercise is derived from the mental rehearsal he used to regain his form and self esteem.

Close your eyes, take a deep breath and, as you release it slowly, let yourself relax into your chair. When you are ready, re-create a scene in which you are competing against your problem opponent. Notice how this feels. Feel yourself warming up and as you do so watch your opponent. How is he preparing himself? Then as he begins to practise look for his strengths. Is he self confident? Strong? Agile? Aggressive? Condescending? Relaxed? Let yourself acknowledge that he has these qualities.

Now become aware how you are feeling. Notice your uncertainties. What advantages does your opponent seem to have over you? What are your shortcomings? Explore and find out how it is that you feel your opponent makes you lose confidence.

Now take a deep breath. Exhale . . . and begin to compete against your opponent . . . and as you do so, you notice that something strange is happening. Through contact or a process of osmosis, you are beginning to absorb some of his positive qualities. Notice how the process occurs.

Steven Paul imagined that every time he touched his opponent's épée with his own he could feel the positive qualities of his opponent flowing into himself like an electric current. Trap-shooter Barbara Lynch, doing the same exercise, saw strength flowing to her in a stream of light from her opponent. For a third athlete, a rainbow made the connection, each colour being a different quality. How do you see this transference of qualities happening between *your* opponent and yourself?

Now focus your attention on one specific quality which you see in your opponent. Perhaps it is aggression. Realise that you recognise this quality in your opponent because you normally possess it yourself and begin to let the quality flow back to you. Imagine the feeling of it filling your body and notice how this quality then infuses your performance.

Take another deep breath and exhale. Now identify another quality which you had 'given' to your opponent. Perhaps this time it is self-confidence. As you continue your mental rehearsal, feel *this* quality flow back into you as well and notice how it too begins to influence your performance. Describe the process out loud – again it is always best to talk your mental rehearsal through with your coach, at least initially.

You should probably work with one quality at a time, making sure you know how it feels, how you hold yourself and how you move when you express that quality in your performance. Better a small substantive change than a magnificent fantasy which has no firm basis. Performed correctly, this exercise allows you to begin reclaiming qualities which you have projected on to your opponent. You change the subjective content of your experience (your response to your opponent) and build new associations through the use of mental imagery. In the end, your opponent is reduced to more human dimensions and you have restored yourself to a position which is a truer reflection of your real ability and gifts.

One of the keystones of our approach is self-knowledge and, through it, self-control. The above and other techniques are designed to give you more conscious control of your mental processes and the means whereby you can direct them in the most efficient and productive manner.

4 *Gestalt dialogue*

If you are having difficulty with a fellow athlete or with your coach (or as a coach with one of your own players), this exercise should help. Again, it is best conducted by a sports psychologist but there's no harm in doing it alone. All you need is two chairs and the ability to act a little.

Sit in one chair and face the other. Now take a minute and imagine that your fellow athlete is sitting in the opposite chair. Notice how he sits and what his mannerisms are. When you have done this, begin a conversation with him as if he were actually there. Tell him what you want from him . . . why you are disappointed, when you get angry with him and how he lets you down.

When you have finished, get up, walk across to the other chair, sit down and *become* your fellow athlete. Think and act the way he does and begin to answer the accusations as if you were him. What are *his* concerns and worries? Why does he act as he does? What does *he* need from this athlete (you) who has complained so bitterly? How has *he* been let down? Give yourself time to imagine the answers and then begin talking as if you were him. How does it feel to talk this way?

Eventually you return to your original chair and continue the conversation, answering 'your fellow athlete's' questions and counter accusations. Move back and forth once or twice until you have a full appreciation of both sides of the issue. Finally, return to the first chair and find some compromise which you are willing to strike, a decision on something you are prepared to do. Try this compromise out in subsequent training sessions, comparing the responses made by your imagined fellow athlete with what actually happens in training. Note which of your suspicions appear to have an element of truth and note which of your characterisations were wrong or distorted. You'll realise that the 'conversation' reflected your *attitudes* about your fellow athlete, not the real person.

These last two exercises help you see how much your attitudes influence you as a competitor, augmenting or hindering your ability to turn in your best performance. Any attitude about yourself, others or your environment is just that: an attitude, not the truth. Treat it as such. After all, however much the other person or the situation may be at fault, your most realistic objective is to change your reaction, rather than change them.

Attitudes about the environment

The third area where attitudes can influence and distort your perception of reality is in dealing with the environment. As we said earlier, an athlete will form an attitude about almost everything to do with his sporting environment, including which shoes feel best for his feet, what colours he likes to wear and in what kind of weather he performs best. As with your opponent or team mate, the environment is something over which you have relatively little control. In the chapter on warming-up we talk about cultivating a positive relationship with the environment, looking for the elements which support you and using them to your advantage, whilst pinpointing the elements which distract you and learning to neutralise their effect.

Sometimes, however, our environment gets the better of us, not because of physical obstruction or interference, but simply because of our attitude. Perhaps you recognise some of these complaints: 'I can't play on clay courts. I tire too quickly.', 'I can't play in a hall with low ceilings because my judgement of distances gets confused.', 'Whenever I compete in front of a big crowd, I lose my confidence.' Any such complaint betrays an attitude where control has been surrendered to the environment and the environmental condition has become an automatic handicap. If, having followed the suggestions in our chapters on warming-up and analytical thinking, you still have such problems with your environment, try one of these exercises:

1 *Likes and wishes*

Take a sheet of paper and, at the top, describe your problem. Then draw a line down the middle and head the left-hand column LIKES and the right-hand one WISHES.

Then think again about the environment that has been causing your problems. When you see it clearly, write down at least three things that you *like* about it. I know you may dread the prospect of playing there but think hard and you'll find something. Maybe the snack bar has exceptional coffee or there is always plenty of hot water in the showers? Write down these 'likes' in the left-hand column. If you can think of more than three, so much the better.

Now in the right-hand column write down three or more wishes you have about the place. It is important to express these thoughts as *wishes* not as dislikes. For example, rather than 'I don't like the lighting.', write: 'I wish the lighting cast less shadow.' Rather than 'The greens are too fast.' write 'I wish I could judge the speed of the greens better.' Instead of 'I don't like the referee.' make it, 'I wish the referee were more observant.'

Once you have done this, you have already begun to get a grip on the situation. First, you have at least three things which you like about the environment which you may never have consciously appreciated before. They may even support you. Secondly, your dislikes have begun to be phrased in terms of possible solutions. You have begun to explore what needs to happen instead of being stuck in a groove.

The next step is to write down a list of as many solutions for each wish as possible. For example, take the wish that the lighting would cast less shadow. How could you combat this? Well, you could mark out the areas where the lighting is worst beforehand, or you might ask if the lighting could be improved, or perhaps you could practise in a poorly-lit hall beforehand. Alternatively you might choose to defend the poorly-lit area first (or to defend the better-lit area first) and so on. Once you have a sense of regaining control, you will be surprised how many solutions will occur to you.

The story then changes. You still may not like the environment but you no longer feel it is controlling you. You are responding to your environment, beginning to initiate new, more productive solutions to old problems and taking responsibility for your encounter with it. You are the cause rather than the effect.

2 *Energising the opposite*

Suppose you have tried everything, but you still hate the idea of having to play on that squash court with the glass wall, where everyone can see you scrabble around in the back corners. You've tried listing what you like about it, you've imagined yourself as invisible, you've practised exercises to keep your concentration on the ball, and still, every time you turn to the back wall, you are inhibited by the spectators. What do you do?

Well, try 'energising the opposite'. Before you go on to the court imagine what it would be like to *love* being the centre of attention. Imagine you *enjoy* people watching your every move. Rehearse yourself playing in this way – how you would think, what you would feel, what you would see, hear and touch. Then go out and play as if it were all true in practice games and then in a match. See yourself as an actor trying a new part for size.

The difference between this and bravado or false calm is two-fold. First you are taking time to plan a specific solution to a specific problem. Secondly, you are doing it with intent. Remember our principle: 'If you know what you are doing, then you can do what you want.' When you energise the opposite you are doing so as a conscious ploy: you are using a chosen technique to deal with an attitude which is counter-productive. When you involve your conscious self in choosing how you respond, you are creating changes which you can maintain. They are not once-off responses over which you have no control and which may or may not work. You are learning how to cultivate a different response to an old situation. You are changing your attitude to the situation and learning how to create and change all of your attitudes.

Gaining energy from attitudes

There is a final point to make about attitudes. Changing attitudes frees additional energy for pursuing new goals and new solutions to old problems. An attitude is an edifice which you built in your mind to sort out information and maintain certain preferred responses. If we didn't have attitudes we would need to learn how to kick a ball or differentiate slice from top spin over and over again. In other words, if your opponent has a heavy top spin then you are quite right to develop an appropriate strategy to cope with it. However, the broader the attitude and the territory of your game which it covers, the more it will dominate your play and the more energy and attention it will hold. The constellation of thoughts, feelings and movements which make up an attitude are bound together by the amount of emotional and attentional energy which went into creating it.

So, when you find ways of changing a long-standing pattern you are not only opening up the possibilities of new response, you are freeing the emotional energy and attention which was being used to maintain that attitude. The ability to hold your attention on new responses increases, the amount of emotional drive for pursuing more appropriate goals is augmented and the necessary physical strength and mobility for learning new patterns of skill is freed. A new self-image can grow out of your past experiences.

8
TEAM SPIRIT

Since it is the coach's job to foster team spirit, this one chapter is addressed to 'you, the coach'. The job is not always easy. Although your team might include a Ray Clemence who says 'Consolidation of defence on the field only happens when the team is together off the field', you'll probably also have a Steve Archibald who will frankly confess that he thinks 'Team spirit is an illusion that you only glimpse when you win.'

How can you convert a collection of average athletes into a team with such understanding that they can beat an unco-ordinated group of individuals who are technically superior? This chapter shows how team meetings and training sessions may be used to generate team spirit, or what we call *synergy*.

The synergistic team

We suspect that many amateur sides have an easier route to the experience of team spirit than top professional teams. A local women's hockey team might spend the Saturday morning together preparing refreshments, the afternoon playing the match, and the early part of the evening sharing the refreshments with their opponents. Furthermore, various members of the team might well meet socially throughout the week. In this way a sense of 'family' spirit is created which is carried onto the pitch.

When Stephen Field talked to members of the Guest Department at the Findhorn Foundation about working together as a group he said 'Don't say, "We must co-operate." Say, "We are one!"' It was clear what he meant but probably only the self-motivated professional would understand such a sentiment.

In chapter 9 we talk about discovery as a motivation for competition. A team offers a path to self-discovery in a community context. Whilst you help each individual to find his or her own identity as an athlete, the group of athletes begins to find its identity as a team. This takes time and involves expressing and resolving conflict so that new appreciation and new

Overleaf: Steve Perryman with the English Football Association Cup – a team triumph.

ideas may form. Gradually, even the most awkward members of your team become hooked on the excitement of group discovery, as it begins to bind the individuals into a perfectly functioning whole. Opponents will find your team unpredictable, brave, fierce and either exciting or alarming, depending on their own degree of unity.

No doubt a modicum of team spirit can evolve without conscious effort on your part and usually does so in the course of training sessions, travel and matches, but, where it is left to chance, athletes who clash too frequently with you or with their team mates will find themselves spinning out to the periphery and thence away. The group you then have left will be relatively harmonious but will lack inventiveness and fire.

Certainly your players don't become a team by being dressed in the same clothes or persuaded to go to bed early the night before an important competition. Such factors may be an expression of team spirit but not its genesis. Unity comes from self-discipline, trust, understanding, caring and freedom of expression. It can't be imposed.

From the time you are appointed, you will set out to learn as much about your squad as you can. You'll help your athletes to appreciate one another's strengths and work with one another's weaknesses. At the same time, you must look for tactics which allow full use of all the available ability and which encourage each individual to develop towards his potential. You have to believe that there *is* a perfect way of using all the potential and skill at your disposal.

A team that discovers the tactics which best suit itself, operates *synergistically*. Synergy is the energy of the perfectly functioning unit and is an energy that is greater than the sum of that unit's individual energies. Team spirit or synergy is an additional strength that may allow a team to beat players who are technically superior to them but who do not work well together. However, if it is to be drawn on in times of stress, it has to be cultivated in training and aroused before the competition begins.

Much of the groundwork involved in creating a synergistic team is best done at team meetings. The correct tactics for the team are discovered through discussion as much as through practical experiment. Properly organised, meetings can be the mental and emotional counterpart to physical training sessions, helping athletes to review, digest and plan, and giving them a chance to explore points of conflict in a safe setting. Even a team that only trains once a week should have a regular time for discussion. Regularity of practice both individually and as a team is as important at the mental and emotional level as it is at the physical.

Team meetings

Team meetings are either for discussion, for a talk, or occasionally a mixture of both. By and large there are three types of meeting:

- 1 *Post-competition discussion meetings*
  Aims: to review and assess performance at the competition.
  to plan for the next competition.

When held: before training on the first day that the team reassembles
after a competition.

The transition from the discussion of the last match to the
discussion of the next one should be clear cut. Sometimes the planning
session can be held on the following day, but it should always take
place at least a day and a training session before the next competition.
Decisions are usually taken at this kind of meeting.

■   2 *Meetings specifically designed to generate team spirit*
Aims: to allow a more wide-ranging and personal discussion of
technical, tactical, social and even political issues that affect the
team.
to introduce new impetus into a season when the way seems
lost.
When held: after a training session, perhaps even away from the
ground altogether. It can be introduced as a positive way of
spending part of an evening when the team is away overnight
or on tour. It may well be the longest and most infrequent of the
three types of meeting. Decisions are not normally taken here.

■   3 *Pre-competition talk meetings*
Aims: to conduct team's emotional warm-up.
When held: immediately preceding a competition. It is a team talk
usually held in the dressing room. There is no discussion and
it is by far the shortest of the three.

All team meetings, whatever their type, can be used to increase team spirit.
As coach, you should plan all meetings in advance and review them
afterwards. The following pages give some advice on preparing, conducting
and reviewing your meetings. This advice applies particularly to discussion
meetings of the type (1) and (2). Hints on conducting pre-competition
meetings (team-talks) are given on p. 132.

Preparing the meeting

The coaching team   All coaches benefit from support in the guise of an
assistant or better still, a full coaching staff. There is then a coaching 'team' to
which the laws of synergy apply equally well. A coach will not only prepare
and analyse meetings with his assistant but will find that his assistant will be
able to interpret the meanings of some athletes that may be difficult for him to
understand. Inevitably, some athletes in the team will empathise with the
coach more than others. An assistant coach provides a healthy balance, an
alternative way of expression and a different way of listening. During the
meetings he will watch whilst the coach is talking and sometimes take over, so
that all athletes are equally able to understand and participate in the team
discussions. Where there is no assistant coach, the captain would normally
take over this interpretive role.

Planning   This does not necessarily need much time but it should be done sitting down and uninterrupted. If the meeting is to be conducted by more than one person (e.g. manager and coach, coach and assistant, coach and captain), it should be planned together. A plan of which only one of you is aware is likely to go awry. It is also unlikely to draw fully on the resources of you both.

Choose your objective carefully   Make sure your objective is clear, even if you choose not to declare it. You may have a subsidiary objective which should also be noted down. For instance, the main objective may be to decide on tactics for the next match, but a subsidiary objective might be to get two players to express differences that they haven't expressed openly.

Write the plan down   A good meeting will contain a strong element of the unexpected and therefore will often not go according to plan, but it is necessary to remember the plan and be aware of how and why the meeting is going off course. Allowing it to go off course should be a deliberate decision, not to be taken lightly.

Once the objective is decided, you must then consider how it is to be achieved. This means taking into account the following factors:

Format   Decide first whether you are going to give a talk or lead a discussion. If it is a *discussion* meeting, will you divide the group? If so, how are you going to divide it? Into pairs? Into threes? Into small groups based on tactical positions? Vary the format. Don't *always* have discussion in a big group, or always in small groups or threes. Occasionally, at a post-match meeting you may decide against discussion altogether and instead give a straightforward talk. As long as you *have* a meeting and there is an established normal format any variation is likely to increase the tempo and degree of participation. Part of your job is to prod players into expressing their creativity. If you want players to be imaginative during the competition, help them to express their imagination during meetings.

As coach, you need to designate the smaller units. Both pairing and grouping can reinforce relationships that are of tactical significance during competition. You won't want them to be the same at every meeting, for athletes should have as many close and personal ties within the team as possible. However, they should be constant enough to give each athlete the sense of belonging to some entity smaller than the team as a whole. In time, each small group develops its own team or 'family' spirit which can contribute to the inspiration and strength of the whole during competition.

Threes are usually random but the small groups (three groups of five rather than five groups of three) should be based on tactical roles (for example, in hockey: forwards, halves and backs; in volleyball: setters, central blockers and spikers). However, for the sake of variation you could sometimes form small groups from new athletes, not-so-new athletes and athletes who have been with the team longest; or simply a grouping that brings together athletes who have had difficulty with each other or do not know each other so well.

Small groups allow each athlete to offset his opinion with a minimum of embarrassment and in a relatively short space of time, thereby becoming immediately involved in the meeting. When the squad itself is small, you won't always need to divide it, but there should still be enough time for everyone to give their opinions. Ricky Villa once said apologetically at a Tottenham meeting: 'I have to say the way I feel or I no feel part of the meeting.' Giving an opinion, even a negative or critical opinion, draws an athlete into the body of the group and allows him to experience more acutely the sense of being part of the team. Young athletes, athletes new to the team, or substitutes who weren't actually involved often have astute observations to make but may hesitate to do so after a more established athlete has expressed his view. You should therefore invite them to speak first, with you and your assistant or captain speaking last.

At the type of meeting devised to boost team spirit, you may decide to divide the group into random threes (threes tend to be more structured and concise than twos and less inhibiting than fours) and ask: 'What can each of you do to improve team spirit and increase communication?' You should then decide how long you will give each person to talk, the best way being to get each person to be 'A', 'B' or 'C' and telling them when it is time to change from 'A' speaking to 'B' speaking and from 'B' to 'C'.

If you are going to lead the meeting with someone else, decide which of you will speak first and who will say what. How can you complement each other and use your different skills and relationship with the athletes to maximum advantage?

Content   Once the format is determined you must decide the content. If it is a discussion meeting decide what questions you are going to ask to set the ball rolling. They must be precise and provoking. The time for 'What did you think of the match?' was immediately after the match, to help the players get back to base. At a post-match discussion you might start by asking: 'What were our objectives?' (if you don't get a ready response your previous meeting was probably inconclusive), or with the statement: 'We decided . . .' and then 'How far did we achieve that objective?' As a general principle, it is best to lead players to give credit before criticism. So you might ask first 'What did we do well?', then 'What did we do wrong?', followed by 'How can we use this information?' However, don't ask exactly the same questions each week.

·   When looking ahead to the next match, the questions may not vary so much. For a ball-game team they will usually be 'What is our prime objective?' (for example, keeping a clean sheet in football or hockey, working for each other, keeping solid, etc.), 'How do we play when we've got the ball?' and 'How do we play when they've got the ball?' In this case, when the team is divided into small tactical groups, you might ask the groups to extend the discussion from 'What is your objective (as a tactical group) in this match?' to 'What do you need from the other two groups?' and 'How will you help the other two groups?' Afterwards, the results of these requests and statements are made by a spokesperson for each group to the others.

Place and time   Having settled the content of the meeting and its form, you must decide where and when the meeting should be held. What place and time suit your objective best? An analytical discussion of the last competition must neither be held too soon nor too long after the event. If held too soon the players won't have completed their emotional review and will be incapable of clear discussion. If too long, they will have lost interest. It should also be held before rather than after a training session, so that decisions that are taken may be put into practice straight away.

When you are to lead a meeting, check the place where the meeting is to be held before anyone arrives. If you want to divide the team into small groups or pairs during part of the meeting, a changing room is not the best place. An untidy room makes for an untidy meeting. Arranging the room to suit your needs not only affects the attitude of the athletes when they arrive but also serves to settle and sharpen your own approach. Remember that noise and interruptions are always distracting and do what you can to find somewhere quiet where you won't be disturbed. This may involve warning people in advance that the meeting is to be held and putting a notice on the door.

Attendance of players   Care may sometimes be needed in deciding who should attend team meetings. In the case of a pre-match talk, it would usually just be the selected team, but any members of the larger squad who might be selected for the following match should be added to this group for the post-match discussion meeting. (Too often in professional football the team that plays on a Saturday will have two or three players that did not attend the review/preview discussion meeting held at the beginning of the week.) Often, injured players should also attend. Not only does this ensure that they continue to be in touch with the spirit of the team but also they frequently have some significant, objective observation to make. Whatever the decision, it is best to tell the athletes why a regular member is absent or formally to welcome someone new. Team spirit builds from meeting to meeting as long as there is continuity.

Arrangement of players   Where players sit in relation to the coach and to one another is an important factor in determining the mood of the meeting. If the meeting is to be primarily discussion, the chairs should be arranged in a circle. Most obviously this is so that everyone taking part may see everyone else. In many team sports, none more so than professional football, athletes are drilled to listen rather than speak whilst the manager is drilled to speak rather than listen. If your athletes are lined up in a row in front of you, especially if they are sitting whilst you stand, it is almost inevitable that every utterance will be directed at you. This may still happen when you are sitting in a circle but then it is easier to deflect. The circle itself seems to embody and inspire an element of unity. Old dances, science fiction and children's stories all refer to the ancient belief that facing inwards and holding hands in a circle keeps evil spirits away. Some sense of this phenomenon seems inherent in the way basketball players will put their hands together in the centre of a tight circle and give a ritual shout at the end of a time-out.

If the meeting is a team *talk* rather than a review or preview discussion, the players don't have to see each other and can sit in any formation, including a row. Furthermore, the coach, who should always sit as part of the circle in a discussion meeting, can stand to address his players when giving a team talk.

When we first went to Tottenham, we found this procedure reversed. At the Monday morning review, the players would sit in a row on benches and the manager and coach would stand back behind a table; whereas the pre-match talks were usually held in the dressing room, the players sitting around beneath their clothes pegs with the manager in the middle of the room (with his back to half of them). This reinforced a tendency for the Monday 'discussions' to be a monologue and the pre-match talk to drift into a drawn-out discussion.

During the meeting

You might adopt the following steps in conducting the meeting:

Attune   Attention can be as scattered prior to a team meeting as it is sometimes before a competition and, in this case, some form of warm-up along the lines suggested in chapter 1 would allow each member of the group to leave aside irrelevant preoccupations and become aware of the group, and the group's reason for meeting.

In an old-fashioned sense, this constitutes dedication to the principles and purposes that unite the individual members. Each person is given time to get in touch with his own sense of responsibility and his reasons for being there. The coach who goads his team into unity by insults, challenges, threats, or scathing appeals to each individual's sense of honour will never quite draw the same degree of commitment from his athletes as will the one who helps each individual athlete to motivate himself. (Of course, plenty of average coaches do neither.) Giving time for your athletes to feel themselves fully present, to make contact with one another, to express personal preoccupations and feelings before the meeting begins is a step in the right direction, however you decide to do it.

Tell the players how the meeting is to proceed   Outline the format and content of the meeting and say how long it will last. (If you are unable to avoid being somewhat drawn off course in terms of format and content, be sure at least to stick to timing. This will pay off in terms of attention at future meetings as the athletes come to trust you.)

Divide the players into groups   When you want to start a discussion in pairs, threes or small groups, it is best to ask the athletes to form these groups *before* you present your prepared questions.

Ask your prepared questions   When asking questions, put them one at a time, giving a time limit for discussion. Make sure that you ask the questions simply, making no comment of your own. If you say what you think first, some of the athletes may not bother to think themselves, believing you have already given 'the answer'. You might ask for a moment's pause before beginning the discussion, so that each athlete first considers his own opinion.

If you write the questions on a blackboard after the discussions have begun, the athletes are more likely to stick to the point. Keep an eye on the time and watch to see which of your athletes in each group are the most and the least involved, being ready to prod the quietest into saying a few words when the large group is formed again. Be prepared to finish this part of the exercise early if talking dies down but otherwise give a two-minute warning before calling a halt.

Bring the team back together to pool ideas At the end of the time allotted to each question, you might ask one member of each group to write down his group's answer. When the team comes back together, the answers to each question can then be read out in turn. Usually this will spark off some new ideas which produce a decision to which all can agree. (Sometimes after a discussion in threes, you might ask athletes to report back to their small groups rather than to the full team circle – but not when you need to guide the team to a decision.)

Conduct circle discussion If you want to draw the best from your athletes in a full circle discussion, consider the following suggestions:

■ *fend off early appeals to your judgement*
The longer you resist giving an opinion during the discussion, the more attention your opinion will command when it is given. You need therefore to be sure not to 'waste' this attention on some minor offshoot of the main discussion but instead to ensure that when you speak you address yourself directly to the central theme, giving a final summary and your opinion, of all that was previously said. However, since there will be many matters raised along the way on which you could well give an insightful opinion, you should note either mentally or on paper these points as they occur to you and give your views when you sum up at the end.

■ *do not get drawn into a protracted dialogue or argument*
Avoid getting drawn into a dialogue or an argument but look around, notice athletes that are silent and prod them into speaking their mind, without giving an answer yourself. Almost invariably you will find someone who will state your own opinion and will draw the fire, allowing you to continue observing. This way, whilst still leading the meeting, you learn more.

■ *watch your athletes*
Watching *instead* of listening is sometimes important. Posture and movement often speak more clearly than words. You gradually learn to interpret the 'body language' of each athlete correctly. This is of particular value to a coach of a game like volleyball who must make snap decisions as to which athletes should be on court and when to substitute. (You might also help and encourage the athletes to make similar observations of one another and then to discuss the interpretation of what they see.)
Look for the athletes who are tense, silent, unsmiling or sitting

somewhat outside the circle. Notice the athletes that talk too much, edging forward to a position where they are unable to notice that others are bored. (These athletes tend to direct all their attention to you.)

- *listen to your athletes*
  It is also important to listen and sometimes intervene. Gradually you will learn to tend the discussion by an apt combination of encouragement and restraint. If it becomes locked in a dialogue, open it out again by suggesting that the two athletes concerned ask the rest of the team how they 'are feeling now' (that is, whether they are bored, interested, sleepy or frustrated, rather than what they *think* about the ideas being endlessly discussed. This will re-involve the other athletes and revive a sense of team spirit.)

- *interrupt chat*
  Notice the difference between talk and chat and cut in decisively to interrupt the chat. Athletes who 'talk' speak their feelings about what is happening at the time; athletes who 'chat' tell anecdotes about other people doing other things somewhere else.

- *watch for emerging themes*
  Sometimes a particular theme comes to the fore during a post-match meeting (for example, 'confidence' or 'honesty') which obviously will require more time for discussion than is then available. Once such a theme has become clear, you should acknowledge the athletes' concern and announce that this will be the subject of a special evening meeting at a later date. You can then guide the current post-match tactical discussion back on course.

- *discourage generalisations*
  When feelings are involved, you should make sure that those speaking start their sentences with 'I . . .', and keep using the present tense. Discourage generalisations such as: 'You . . .', 'We . . .', 'People . . .', 'The midfield . . .', etc., and ask the speaker to be specific. I remember one Tottenham meeting when a player asked: 'How do we get to believe in ourselves?' It would have been interesting to ask him to change his sentence to 'How do *I* get to believe in ourselves?' (emphasising that it is *his* fantasy that there is a general lack of belief) and then, exploring a deeper level, to change it to 'How do I get to believe in *myself?*' However, he immediately had one or two forceful replies beginning 'We should . . .' This locution holds the same doubtful assumption and such a statement has to be challenged by asking 'All right, but what are *you* going to do?' And then, as a further step, 'What will I *see* you do?' Once one athlete has made such a precise commitment, the mist begins to clear and the shift from discussion towards action begins to take place.

- *remember the axiom: 'Behind every question there is a statement'*
  Players tend to slow down a discussion by asking questions, often to

the coach but also to other athletes. Much time can be lost guessing why the question has been asked and hazarding suitable answers. If you remember the axiom: 'Behind every question is a statement', and ask the questioner first to make a statement in the present tense beginning with 'I . . .', useful discussion will usually follow. (Sentences beginning 'I wonder why . . .' don't count!)

■ *bring the meeting to a positive conclusion*
When you feel that the discussion is becoming repetitive and notice that the allotted time is almost passed, begin to draw things to a close. Rather than ask: 'So, what is the conclusion?', however, it is better to say 'It seems that the conclusion is . . .' and allow a moment for deeply-felt amendments to be made. Should the discussion threaten to break out again, it is probably time to stand up and call a halt.

The final words on tactics are yours

Now that each athlete has invested energy in the discussion, you will have their complete attention and, having listened to everyone else, you will see how to link your own opinion with the views already expressed. When the discussion has been inconclusive or your own views are at complete variance with the team's, you may need to impose a decision for a trial period. (In such cases it is best to ask athletes to restate your decision, to make sure it has been properly understood.)

Whatever the decisions, you would do well to write them up on a blackboard. Although this may have dreary connotations for some athletes, these can be changed with a little patience. Eventually, the athletes will recognise the value of having the decisions crystal clear and will gain a sense of each discussion meeting leading to a purposeful conclusion, instead of being the release of so much impressionistic hot air. Even the most distracted non-verbal athlete in the team will be aware of the message and the theme of the week and, if the decisions are left on the blackboard until the next match, they become slogans which the players will hear echoed and will themselves repeat in training.

Additional techniques for discussion meetings

Various exercises or games may be used to stimulate discussion and generate team spirit. Here are a few:

● 1 *Circle checks*
When the group comprises not more than a dozen athletes and the discussion is becoming repetitive and confused, you can break in and ask for a 'circle check'. Each person in turn then makes a one-sentence statement of his view without anyone giving him a direct response. Very often a surprisingly clear common opinion then emerges.

● 2 *Listing strengths and weaknesses*
To introduce an initial discussion on loss of confidence and team spirit,

ask athletes to call out their doubts about the team's ability or the weaknesses they perceive and write these on the blackboard. Then ask them to call out the strengths that they still feel the team possesses and write these up too. It is possible that once the doubts have been made specific, remedies will be easier to find. The doubts of one athlete may find a ready answer from another. A plan of action can be built which also capitalises on the team's perceived strengths.

3 *Drawing out the individual*

A more probing approach to loss of confidence is as follows. When an athlete says that he has no confidence in the team, lead him first to say which aspect of his *own* game he wants to improve and then to become aware of which athlete or athletes specifically it is in whom he has no confidence. He should then be asked to think of one strength that person has which he appreciates and one thing that that person is capable of doing which would improve the confidence he has in him. Finally, he should be asked to notice any tactical connection there might be between the improvement he wants from the other athlete and the improvement that he wants from himself.

Before asking these questions, you might see if there are any other athletes feeling a lack of confidence in 'the team'. Were you then to ask all such athletes to write down the answers to each question and to give them to you afterwards, you could devise a follow-up exercise for a later session which would give an opportunity for the critical, self-critical and appreciative thoughts to be expressed openly. You may of course choose to institute such an exercise directly, without asking for the comments to be written down. Either way, you would learn something about the athletes concerned and might well find clues as to tactical changes which would improve the team's morale.

4 *Encouraging 'silent' athletes*

If you realise that an otherwise animated discussion has only involved half of the athletes in the circle, call a halt and ask each person who hasn't talked to stand up and choose one who has talked already. Ask the pairs to sit together in different parts of the room and ask the 'silent' athlete to tell the 'talkative' one his view on the subject being discussed. If each athlete has been asked to make a decision or commitment of some sort, let them comment on their partner's decisions.

5 *Encouraging honesty*

There was a stage during the 1982/3 season when some Tottenham players felt that others weren't 'being honest' in the discussion meetings. Certainly many found it easier to make generalised statements about the team rather than to admit to a lack of confidence in themselves. If such athletes are to assess their own performance realistically and are to decide to work on certain aspects of it, they need to be encouraged to do this in a 'safer' situation than the large circle.

If you have about fifteen athletes, ask them to number off from one to five around the circle and then tell all the ones to form one group, all the twos another, and so on, so that the athletes end up in random groups of three. (Groups of four are too large for this exercise. If you have extra athletes, form a group with them yourself.) Ask each three to settle which of them is to be 'A', 'B' and 'C' and then tell 'A' he has three minutes to say what pleases him about his performance and what it is that he is going to improve. 'B' and 'C' listen without any comment, although, towards the end of the time they may prompt 'A' to say more by asking a question. At the end of three minutes, you call 'Time!' and 'B' goes through the same procedure, with 'A' and 'C' listening. When all three have had their three minutes, give another five minutes for feedback between the three of them. At the end of that five minutes, bring the athletes back and go round the circle, each athlete stating one thing that he is going to improve.

Either you or your assistant should note these resolutions and later discuss with each athlete how he can best achieve his objective in terms of training.

6 *Brain-storming*
At more leisurely meetings, such as those conducted at the beginning of the season or on evenings prior to a match, the solution to a long-standing problem can sometimes be found by 'brain-storming'. You present the problem (for example, 'How can I increase team spirit?'). For the next ten minutes, the athletes suspend all normal analytical patterns of thought and judgement, let their imagination flow freely and throw out ideas. Of these, you choose two or three that you like. The athletes then suggest how you might put each of your chosen ideas into practice. Finally you choose one solution that you like and ask yourself what, if anything, keeps you from acting on it and what you can do about that. You then make a commitment to the team as to when you will put the solution into effect.

7 *I see . . . I imagine . . . and that makes me feel . . .*
This game, described earlier, can be played first in the ordinary way, athletes saying what they notice and feel about other members of the team at the time. Then it might be played in terms of their perception of one another's performance in competition. In this case it is played in the past tense. Provided that there is plenty of time left for feedback between individuals at the end of the game, a number of mis-understandings should be dispelled.

8 *'What I would do if I were coach for the next seven days.'*
Let the small groups discuss this proposition for twenty minutes and then ask a spokesperson from each group to feed back ideas to the main group. This allows dissatisfaction to be expressed creatively and for individuals to get feedback and new perceptions from other members of their small groups.

9 *'As if . . .' discussions*
Ask every member of the team to imagine that they are someone within

their particular sport whom they greatly respect. Then divide into random groups of four (count one to three around the circle, if there are twelve athletes and put ones together, twos together and threes together), and spend ten minutes discussing their *own* strengths and weaknesses with the other two people in the group *as if* they were the persons they admire but talking about themselves in the third person. Set a scene for them before they begin (for example, they might be in the clubhouse, in the pub, or at one of their houses just after a competition) and make sure each group acts out a conversation and does not speak strictly in turn.

10 *'Wise person' exercise*

The following psychosynthesis exercise can be used to help your athletes each to answer the question: 'What can I do to increase team spirit?' Such an exercise would allow athletes to relax and retreat into themselves for a while after a long period of interpersonal exercises, providing a dynamic contrast to rational left-brain discussion.

You ask your athletes to lie on the floor, close their eyes and relax following your instructions. You then ask them to imagine they are in a field close to a mountain. Leading the exercise slowly, helping them to visualise as clearly as possible, you ask them to leave the field and climb the mountain until they see some sort of a building or shelter on the top. They go inside. There they see a wise old person and ask the question: 'What can I do to increase team spirit?' They should remember uncritically the first reply they 'hear'. You then lead them back down the mountain to the field and eventually back to the room. Ask them to talk about the exercise in pairs before coming back together for discussion with the squad.

This exercise may be used at other times to provide answers to further questions. It allows an appeal to be made to the intuitive right hemisphere of the brain, rather than to the logical left hemisphere.

11 *Unfinished business*

'Is there any unfinished business?' is a question you might well ask before closing any discussion meeting. Athletes who sit on resentments and then express them to others after the meeting is over are, as we said in chapter 5, a drain on team spirit. This doesn't necessarily mean that the meeting has to go into a new phase, just as it was about to end. All that you ask is that any resentment (or for that matter any appreciation) left unsaid should be spoken. The athlete who speaks maintains his integrity as a member of the team and is then free to explore the matter further after the meeting.

12 *Making a final statement*

Having dealt with the question of unfinished business, a final circle check on the lines of 'How I am feeling now' gives each athlete a chance to summarise his experience and indirectly affirm his membership of the team. Each statement should be very brief and neither invite nor receive any form of discussion.

- 13 *Appreciations*
  One direct way of raising team spirit is to ask each athlete to consider
  the athlete on his right and, going around the circle, briefly express one
  thing that he appreciates about this neighbour either as a person, as a
  team member or as an individual performer. This exercise is best used
  at the very end of a meeting. A variation is to form random small
  groups (of about five athletes) and ask each person to give a one-line
  appreciation of every other person in the group. You should insist that
  appreciations are always statements and that there be no discussion as
  or after they are made. One easy way of enforcing this procedure is to
  pass some object around the circle, with the instruction that only the
  athlete holding the object is entitled to speak. Appreciation exercises
  tend to increase both caring and confidence between athletes.
      Another variation that might be used earlier on in the meeting is the
  'appreciation sandwich'. This takes longer (unless it is performed in
  small groups, rather than the whole circle) and involves each athlete
  thinking of *two* appreciations and one 'request' to make of his
  neighbour. Again, these are expressed around the circle, each athlete
  giving his first appreciation, his request and his second appreciation to
  his neighbour in turn.

The above suggestions are some ways in which you can encourage your
players to express themselves clearly and take responsibility for their beliefs
and feelings during discussion meetings. Together, the athletes create a sense
of safety and freedom, learning to trust one another and, more importantly,
to trust themselves. Expressing his feelings clearly helps the athlete further
towards realising his potential both as an athlete and as a member of the team.

As a coach, you are an educator, one who 'leads out', not one who
directs. Were you always to sit your athletes in rows and direct the
proceedings too obviously, they might behave like a class of bored children,
unwilling to take responsibility for their actions and experience. There is no
point in imposing a set of tactics that the athletes are unable to understand.
Better to be patient and ask questions that will prompt discovery. Essentially,
though, it is a question of caring for the athletes. Then they draw closer,
speak more easily, dare to try new things and give more of themselves. In fact,
your real responsibility is to provide a context, create an atmosphere in which
some unique discovery may occur. You are not solely responsible for that
discovery nor can you *always* know in advance what it will be.

After the discussion meeting/During the week

Ideally, both coaches and athletes would review a meeting just as we suggest
they review a match. In fact, if the job were done thoroughly, not only the
decisions but also personal observations, impressions and new ideas would
be written down afterwards and kept for future reference. This would
strengthen continuity and the sense of progress being made. Discussions
would become less repetitive and easier to start.

When the main decision of the meeting (which may be expressed as a *slogan,* an *evocative word* or an *affirmation)* is left on the board, the tactically-determined small groups should be encouraged to meet again later to determine how they specifically will carry it through. How must each group interpret the decision, for instance, when they are attacking or when they are defending? In the meantime, the training sessions should be planned in a way that develops the required qualities, and, when practice competitions are held, each athlete's performance can be scored in terms of his success at playing in the required manner. These analyses will then be the subject of further short meetings prior to training.

All this helps the individual athlete to see how he personally can help the team towards its objective. It is important that he is clear about this at least the night before the match. The more clearly he sees his way forward, the more confident his approach.

When the match is over, the procedure should be reversed. Both the individual athletes and their small groups should consider how far they reached their objectives in the agreed way and see what lessons there are to be learned.

Having had an initial discussion early in the week, some adjustments may have to be made after the first training session or because of injuries. However, as the season progresses and the week goes by there should be a decreasing need for discussion and more for talk. You then remind the team of the objective that was agreed together and the means by which that objective is to be reached until, at the final pre-match talk, the memory of their initial decision-making process is used as an invocation or rallying call to spur the players on. The most effective pre-match pep-talk is not a tirade but an inspiring reminder of all that binds the players together.

After the meeting at the start of the season, when the team's overall objective is established, the individual motivations of the players should be written down and not forgotten. It helps to know as much about each athlete's background as possible and to be aware of events in each athlete's current life which make strong demands on his attention. Other factors in their lives might change and affect their relationship to the team. This process of 'personal sharing' continues in and out of meetings throughout the season. As trust develops, athletes begin to meet each other in other places and talk about things other than their sport. From time to time at subsequent meetings you should have a circle check to find out if anything has changed. In fact, each season has its pattern and there are usually key moments when a review and re-evaluation of the *team*'s long-term goals have to be made. What is the next step? Are the goals still exactly the same?

The pre-competition meeting

In this type of meeting the coach talks and the athletes listen. You should give an absolute minimum of new information. Repeat in the clearest and most direct way the tactics decided at the discussion meeting earlier in the week and practised at subsequent training sessions. A good pre-competition team talk is a touchstone for evoking team spirit.

In summary, such a talk can:

(i) eliminate all remaining confusion and distraction

(ii) calm athletes who are too anxious

(iii) arouse athletes who are too relaxed

(iv) unite all athletes in the sense of belonging to an entity that is greater than the sum of their individual selves

The effectiveness of such a talk largely depends therefore on the amount of time and care that you have invested in earlier team discussions.

Remember that the mental warming-up should precede the emotional and physical. Ideally it is completed before the day of the match but if you still have essential information to impart, make sure you keep it simple and give it at the start of your talk. Once you have moved into the emotional warm-up do not turn back to more information or the tension will be lost. This applies equally before the competition and at any break during the competition. At Tottenham, the coach had a more mental approach than the manager. We always felt that the pre-match and half-time talks were more effective when the coach, Peter Shreeve, gave his analysis before the manager gave the 'emotional lift'. When the process was reversed or when additional pieces of information were added at the end, the effect of the emotional build-up was lost.

Training sessions

You can inspire team spirit during training as well as at meetings. This is also a time to observe how athletes relate to one another in their tactical decisions, gestures or words, and to organise small group and pair exercises accordingly. Once again, any decision as to which athletes work together will be partly designed to improve the level of concern and intuitive understanding between them. Bear the following points in mind when planning training sessions.

Make the theme ring loud in the athletes' minds   Training sessions should be planned according to the decisions taken at the start of the week. The earlier those decisions are made, the longer there is to reinforce them during training. As coach, you should take responsibility for the team winning and give the athletes the responsibility of performing in a way that you believe is most likely to result in victory. The athletes must be convinced that the theme or the attitude is more important than the result. Let the athletes know that they will not be judged by the result but by how far they played in the manner that was agreed. If your hockey team's priority is to keep a clean sheet, any practice match should be scored according to defensive tackles rather than goals. This improves defensive play, increases confidence as players realise they are to be judged on something within their control and provides the stimulus and fun of a different approach.

Giving his view on an unexpected defeat, Tony Galvin once said at a Tottenham meeting that the team had begun well, playing 'solid' as agreed, but eventually had panicked because they had scored no goals. The theme had been forgotten and the team regressed to the old ingrained instruction 'You must score goals.' The truth is that the pressure to win is so great that unless the chosen theme is crystal clear the team *will* panic and the theme will be forgotten. As coach, therefore, you have to make the theme 'louder' in the athletes' minds than the ingrained message 'Win! You have to win!'

You can begin to do this by:
(i) deciding the theme early in the week
(ii) making sure each individual athlete knows what is required of him and on what he is to be judged
(iii) emphasising the theme daily before and during training
(iv) having analyses done of how well each athlete plays according to the theme during practice

Ensure regular attendance You should also try to ensure regular attendance at training sessions. This is as important as attendance at meetings if trust and respect are to grow between athletes. Even an athlete who is injured should attend all the sessions that he can. In doing so, he is able to retain much of the intuitive understanding that links him with other athletes and can continue to contribute his moral support. Once recovered from the injury, his re-absorption into the team will be much quicker (this is particularly important for clubs without a large number of reserves). Not only may there be certain facets of his play that he can continue to work on (the rest he can practise with mental rehearsal) but there will also be ways in which he can help others. In volleyball, he may feed the balls for you in certain drills, make analyses or shout encouragement during a match. His presence can be an inspiration to the rest of the team. Athletes with whom he has a particularly close tactical link will find his enforced objective observation of their performance particularly valuable.

At the same time, the team can help the injured athlete. Being with his team and in touch with its team spirit is in itself a healing experience. If you mention the athlete and his injury at the beginning of a training session, the team's momentary act of together focusing care and attention on him may even hasten the healing process.

Conduct imaginative exercises Imaginative exercises that highlight some point made at the previous meeting immediately generate enjoyment and an element of team spirit. In fact, you should also ensure that each athlete regularly experiences those elements of his sport that he most enjoys. This improves his confidence and indirectly improves the confidence of the rest of the team.

For instance, it is possible to play-out an *ideal model* visualisation with the whole team taking part. At Tottenham, Ossie Ardiles was universally regarded as a confident, aware organiser on the field. Early in the 1982/3 season, when he was playing on loan to the Paris club, St Etienne, Tottenham players often referred to him at team meetings and to the confidence he used to impart. A way of experiencing and regaining a sense of confidence and team awareness is to act out an '*as if* . . .' visualisation whereby each player pretends during a short practice game that *he* is someone the whole team considers to be confident, like Ossie Ardiles, with the winning side being the one whose players most succeed in the imitation, not the side scoring the most goals. Afterwards the players would need a chance to express their experience of the exercise, if the most is to be gained from it.

Combat depression with simple tasks   When your athletes are performing consistently well, you can expect them to be inventive, exciting and forever trying the unexpected. The basic pattern, the underlying rules, the agreed *slogans* are learned and completely absorbed so that the performance becomes a succession of imaginative variations on a theme. However, when confidence has taken a severe knock and the team threatens to revert into a disjointed group of individuals, it is best to reaffirm and practise the most obvious basic principles, going back to exercises you used when introducing those principles in early days. As with an athlete overcome with anxiety, you need to divert the team's attention from the overall depressing picture to a specific task that they can perform confidently. It is even better if you can arrange for these performances to be evaluated statistically. This way the intuitive creative flights of fancy will be given a rest and the basic skills on which they depend will be strengthened.

Team spirit and the individual

Team spirit is highest when all athletes train individually as well as together at regular training sessions. Each athlete should aim to reach his own potential, working at an additional training programme designed specifically to improve his weaknesses. Athletes of average ability who train well alone contribute more to team spirit than do any of the star players who will not do additional training.

You can best inspire team spirit in individual athletes if you:

■   *are consistent*
    Team spirit would be reduced by diminished trust in your own clarity of intent. If you change systems or athletes or the roles of the athletes you use too often, there will be a loss of confidence, which will draw the athletes' attention away from the team and back into themselves.

■   *talk to individual players*
    All players need individual attention, whether they show this outwardly or not. When you talk to athletes individually, tell them in advance how long you have to spend with them and then guide them to speaking first. Before you comment on their performance, find out their own assessment and what objectives they have. You may well find that you are given an easy lead to a criticism that you want to make.

■   *make only just and positive criticisms*
    As far as possible, back your criticism with statistics. Keeping a record of specific elements of an individual's performance will prevent you maintaining out-of-date negative attitudes. If you ever catch yourself saying about one of your athletes 'He always . . .' make sure that you get someone to check that aspect of his performance on the next

possible occasion. The expression 'holding someone in a negative thought-form' means just that: blocking that person's development by constantly talking about their fault, making it harder for them to change if your criticism holds an element of truth. Statistics provide a neutral basis for discussion and for planning a way to improve.

Sometimes mistakes can be made just through inattention. Keith Burkinshaw once complained that a certain player had been booked 'yet again' for arguing with the referee. It was true that this player had been frequently booked the previous season but Keith only had to look on the board on his wall to realise that, although it was already mid-April, this was the first occasion in the whole of that season that the player had been booked. Old thought-forms die hard.

- *watch out for loss of confidence*
Loss of confidence can be a drain on team spirit. It is similar to anxiety in that it inhibits creative expression and communication with other members of the team. Both engender mental (and to some extent physical) paralysis so that the athlete no longer knows clearly what he is trying to do. An athlete without confidence in himself can't communicate with the rest of the team. It is then your job to help him rediscover his sense of security and to re-establish the invisible links he had with other athletes. An athlete who professes confidence in himself but none in the team also isolates himself and needs your attention. He, too, is a drain on team spirit. His attitude is closed and negative and, not seeing the team's strength, he won't play to it.

You could help each of these athletes in a different way. The one who has lost confidence in the team should first be encouraged to state his feelings more specifically at a team meeting. The athlete who has lost confidence in himself needs to speak to you alone and identify specific situations which provoke these feelings. He must then be helped to evolve a plan of action for dealing with such situations when they next occur. The plan will embody a number of targets along the way which will give him a sense of progressing towards the time when he will be able to cope. Make sure he is clear about what is expected of him, and on what he will be judged. Once he learns that he can trust you to judge him in this way and provided you have not asked him to play in a manner beyond his ability, his confidence will return.

- *maintain contact with reserve, substitute or injured athletes*
If you have reserve, substitute or injured athletes, make sure you maintain personal contact with them. It is harder for them to get out of themselves, to step forward and offer their energy to the team and yet, if there is the likelihood of them being in the team one day, that aspect of their game also needs practising. When they can't actually play as part of the team, they should watch the team performing as often as possible and imagine the feeling of taking part, gaining a sense of the pattern of play.

■ *ensure all athletes work equally hard*
In ball-game sports, athletes whose main function is to attack often gain much of the limelight, so that this aspect of their play can become over-emphasised, even in their own perception. When their own team have possession of the ball, they rightly look to receiving support or 'service' from other athletes in the team. However, team spirit can be threatened if you don't help these same athletes to consider their role as defenders, when the opposition have the ball and *they* have the opportunity to support and serve.

■ *ensure positive talk*
In most sports, keeping in touch verbally helps maintain team spirit when intense pressure might otherwise cause individual players to retreat into themselves or quarrel with others. Four distinct types of talking can be identified:
    (i) destructive criticism, usually given just after someone has made a mistake
    (ii) demands: 'Give it to me!', 'Over here!', 'Quick!', etc.
    (iii) positive instructions, as might be given by an athlete who is better placed to see than his team mate who is about to act
    (iv) encouragement: not just congratulations after the event but words which put an extra yard on a volleyball dive or add extra power to an attacking run in football
Obviously, the third and fourth types are the most inspiring, whilst the first type should be sharply discouraged.

9
COMPETITION AND MOTIVATION

Here, John Syer describes how his personal view of competition gradually changed. He concludes that the challenge of competition can either push us to reach some externally imposed standard or help us to discover our potential.

Christopher Connolly then goes on to explain how we make the transition from being motivated by the opinions, rewards or threatened reprisals of others to become genuine self-starters.

A personal view of competition

As a boy at boarding school, the prospect of a spring term Saturday morning was so exciting that it was almost a physical event. The day seemed to have both a colour – a pale primrose yellow – and a smell. The smell is easier to explain than the colour, for it was definitely that of a newly-rolled hockey pitch, and indeed my excitement was inseparably linked with the sight of the waiting field, the freshly painted lines, the sturdy white goals, the magic semi-circles and the flags flapping idly at each corner.

Hockey was more absorbing than anything else in the world and my Indian hockey stick was as familiar as a close friend. Looking back, it seems now that the pleasure I found in the game was entirely kinaesthetic – the feeling of my own speed, strength, agility and control – and had little to do with anyone else.

In the army, during my National Service, it was different. I had the good fortune to be posted to Edinburgh at the same time as one or two fine players with whom I was able to practise, week in, week out. Gradually I learned to appreciate another dimension of the game, that of team spirit, but within eighteen months I was demobbed and I found myself spending the next three years in France and Algeria, without playing much sport at all.

I took up volleyball at Edinburgh University. Someone stole my hockey boots at a stage when I was discouraged with my performance and, seeing a notice appealing for people to join the volleyball team, I felt a surge of nostalgia for a particular beach in Algeria. The next fifteen years of my life were all volleyball – first Edinburgh University, then the London-based

Tug-of-war – a common resolve, but each may be motivated differently.

139

British team as a player and finally coaching the Scottish senior men's team whilst tending the growth of the Scottish Volleyball Association.

Initially these were all good times that touched their heights when a much-practised tactic worked perfectly, when I experienced an intuitive connection with all the other members of the team or in those occasional moments of 'peak experience' where everything was crystal clear and had a momentum of its own. The teams I played for and coached were like families. Our training sessions were as enjoyable as the matches and the times we spent together travelling, first around Scotland and then further and further abroad, were a natural extension of the eating, drinking and singing sessions we enjoyed after our matches.

Then gradually negativity crept in. I noticed anger, frustration and anxiety in other players and teams and eventually came to recognise these feelings in myself. Sometimes the price seemed too high and, after two or three years of hearing the Edinburgh University women's team captain tell me I should attend yoga classes to help me calm down and expand my horizons, I decided to give it a try.

A new cycle seemed to begin. I met new people, visited the Findhorn Foundation in the north of Scotland and decided to stay. Some time later I heard of Timothy Gallwey and his concept of 'Yoga Tennis', understanding from the person who described it to me that the idea was to turn one's attention away from anxieties and frustrations and focus on playing beautifully for its own sake. Very soon I was back in business and formed a Findhorn volleyball team, attempting to put these new ideas into practice. It was a team of amateur philosophers and we had a series of long meetings to discuss our new ideas, taping them because we felt they were so exciting.

It didn't quite work out. We entered the local league with much enthusiasm but not winning a single game distracted most of us from the intention of ignoring the opposition and playing beautifully. Besides, it was hard to convince ourselves that we *were* playing beautifully when the opposition left us standing (or even sitting) with their barrage of spikes through the heart of our defence. Players attended training sessions less regularly and it began to be difficult to put a side together for the following Saturday's match.

It was then that I finally obtained a copy of Gallwey's book, *The Inner Game of Tennis* (London House, 1974, Cape, 1975), and found to my surprise that Gallwey had been through a similar cycle: 'I became non-competitive. Instead of trying to win, I decided to attempt only to play beautifully and excellently . . . absorbed solely in achieving excellence for its own sake. But something was missing. I didn't experience a desire to win and, as a result, I often lacked the necessary determination . . .'

As I read on, I felt myself waking up. *This* was what I'd been seeking for a long time. So much of my volleyball experience seemed to acquire new meaning and I felt that I had to go to California, meet Timothy Gallwey, and write 'The Inner Game of Volleyball'. I created and acted on the opportunity of going to America, helping to initiate a staff exchange programme between the Findhorn Foundation and the Esalen Institute. Within four months I was on the plane heading for the Esalen Sports Institute and Timothy Gallwey. There were more surprises to come.

The Esalen Sports Institute was not at Esalen, and it was not even any longer an office in San Francisco . . . and Timothy Gallwey was unobtainable. I found myself an hour's drive from the nearest town and gardening four days a week in exchange for my salary. At weekends I attended workshops and had my first introduction to gestalt therapy and related human potential disciplines. It was late February, I'd arrived from Scotland, the sun was warm, the sparkling sea alive with whales and the eucalyptus trees swarming with enormous monarch butterflies. Later I was to meet Michael Murphy, Bob Kriegel, Mike Spino and Ken Dychtwald, but for the time being I was distracted, relaxed and let things ride.

I started to read one of Fritz Perls' books, *Gestalt Therapy* (Perls, Hefferline and Goodman, Penguin, 1951). One day I came across the sentence: 'The bother with neurotic competitiveness is not the competition but the fact that the competitor is not interested in the game.' I laid down the book and two thoughts came to mind: firstly, if Perls refers to a 'neurotic competitiveness', he must believe there is some sort of competitiveness that is *not* neurotic, whereas in our Findhorn attempts to 'play beautifully' we had considered competitiveness to be the source of all that is negative in sport; secondly, if the competitor is not interested in the game, what *is* he interested in?

I remembered Gallwey's story of losing the final of the All American Junior Championships when he was fifteen because, at two sets to love up, he suddenly felt sorry for the eighteen-year-old he was about to beat. Gallwey points out: 'If I assume that I am making myself more worthy of respect by winning, then I must believe, consciously or unconsciously, that by defeating someone, I am making him less worthy of respect.'

So this was the answer to my question. A competitor who is not interested in the game is interested in gaining attention and respect. He wants to prove himself to be something that he wants to be or that he thinks he ought to be, and this can be termed 'neurotic competitiveness'.

And at last I understood. Competitiveness is *not* necessarily neurotic. A true competitor, a competitor who is creative and who *is* interested in the game, is not competing to prove he is something he feels he should be, but to find out *who he really is*, in the faith that whoever or whatever that turns out to be it will be unique and perfect.

Gallwey's own breakthrough came when his father, confronted with Gallwey's original philosophy of playing perfectly and ignoring the opposition, asked why, in that case, the surfer waits for the big wave. Gallwey had to answer: 'It is only against the big waves that the surfer is required to use all his skill, all his courage and concentration to overcome; only then can he realise the true limits of his capacities. At that point he often slips into a superconscious state and attains his peak. In other words, the more challenging the obstacle he faces, the greater the opportunity for the surfer to discover and extend his true potential.'

George Leonard, another Esalen course leader, writing about the martial art 'aikido' in his book *The Ultimate Athlete* (Avon, 1974), says: 'Every aikidoist faces the problem of finding a good practice partner, one who will attack with real intent. The greatest gift the aikidoist can receive from his partner is the clean true attack, the blow that, unless blocked, or avoided, will strike home with real effect. This gift of energy can be turned into a lovely dance in which neither partner is hurt and both are joined. The half-hearted attack is harder to deal with and more likely to lead to injury.'

Maintaining this simile of dance, Leonard writes about the famous American football player O. J. Simpson: 'To dance, O.J. needs worthy opponents; it is in fact their excellence and their full commitment to stop him that forces his dance to higher levels . . . He needs a physical and psychological context to his dance . . .'

Fritz Perls points out that conflict or competition can be the point of creative discovery in art, scientific theorising and sport. He goes on to talk about the possible creative value that might emerge if conflict is allowed to arise in a group or team discussion. This would apply equally in business or a team tactics meeting. 'Conflict can be a collaboration going beyond what is intended, towards a new figure altogether . . . The more sharply a group differ and have it out, the more likely they are to produce collectively an idea better than any of them had individually. So in games it is the competition that makes the players surpass themselves.'

Brent Rushall, the Canadian sports psychologist, observes: 'More effort and intensity is put into competition than into training . . . Athletes are able to discern that they have something "extra" which can be used in competitive circumstances.'

The concept of some extra energy becoming available at the creative moment when each part of an individual or each member of a team fully contributes his own energy to the whole, is that of synergy, as we discussed in chapter 8. The point made here is that an element of conflict is necessary if something new is to be created or discovered. However, the process does depend on the person or the group concerned having faith in the fact that whatever is discovered will be perfect. It can take time and experience to acquire such faith.

We have discussed ways in which this faith can be generated within a team. We should now spend a little time considering the process in terms of the individual athlete and in what sense his acquisition of faith in himself is itself the true genesis of his motivation.

Motivation

What is motivation? How does it work? How can I motivate myself? How can I motivate the members of my team more? Coaches and athletes often ask us these and other related questions.

Coaches in particular seem to be plagued by such problems. A common statement from coaches runs something like this: 'I have this athlete. He is young. He is built right for his sport. He has tremendous gifts and ability. When he applies himself, he works wonders. And yet he is only there part of the time. I can only get 50% of his ability out of him. If I say the wrong thing, then he goes away completely.', or 'He only shows up five minutes before training and is the first one away home.', or 'If I push him, he becomes surly and unco-operative.', or 'If I give in too much, he thinks he is on easy street and doesn't perform at all.'

The self-starting athlete, the one who is there, has the desire to fulfil his potential and is co-operative, is the coach's dream. We all look for that kind of athlete since he is so easy to teach. The problem is that very often the most gifted athlete is the one with the problems. He is the one inclined to be unpredictable and tetchy. When on form, he is brilliant. When off form, he can be the most frustrating individual in the world, both within and outside the sports situation.

So, again, what is motivation? It has been the subject of many theories, tests and measurements but, since this book is not about tests and measurements and since theories are only of use in so far as they indicate

Competition enables athletes to 'surpass themselves'. Dorando Pietri, Italy, who finished first in the 1908 Olympics Marathon but was not declared the winner because he was helped over the line by officials – perhaps showing the effects of a true competitive spirit?

specific techniques, we hesitated to write about motivation. This then is a section to take or to leave. If the following theory makes sense to you, use it as a model for reflecting on what motivates you or your players. If it doesn't make sense, throw it out. When Diana Whitmore lectures on psychosynthesis, she has a sentence in the corner of the blackboard that she never rubs out: THIS IS NOT THE TRUTH. What follows is not 'the truth' but it is a theory that you may be able to relate to your experience.

Traditional models of motivation centre around rewards and punishment or, in behaviouristic terms, 'positive' or 'negative reinforcement'. If you are a rat in a maze and are rewarded with food for finding the right path, then, because you are rewarded with something that you *want*, you learn to find the right path quickly and follow it regularly. On the other hand, if you travel down the wrong part of the maze, you receive an electric shock. You then stop going in that direction because you *don't want* an electric shock. The operative word here is 'want'.

This traditional 'want' and 'don't want' model can be rephrased into something a little more human and sophisticated: 'achievement' and 'avoidance'. Such a model is often used in sport.

It is said that an athlete is motivated either by offering him what he wants (should he succeed) or by threatening him with what he wants to avoid (should he fail). Through success, he may achieve recognition by his coach, team mates and family; fame through public exposure, press and television; money through good contracts, promotions and good job offers; and approval from his coach, his peer group, his parents and his spouse. It might also be realised that somewhere amongst such rewards are self-esteem and a sense of the athlete reaching his potential but such factors are difficult to assess and are assumed to be of secondary significance.

According to the same model, avoidance evolves from the threat of punishment in the form of criticism, verbal chastisement, removal from the first team, pain, exhaustion in competition (leading to still harder training); disapproval from the coach, close friends and the public; embarrassment (in front of the public or friends); loss of past achievements – of standing in league tables, of contract, of money and of fame. Loss of self-esteem and disappointment at not fulfilling potential may be mentioned, but, again, being difficult to assess, such factors are often shuffled aside.

Both these theories of motivation are based on the 'desire element'. The cruder negative and positive reinforcement model suggests that the coach finds something which the athlete wants or fears, in order to influence the way in which that athlete will behave. In the achievement and avoidance model, the athlete himself is seen as seeking or avoiding something in his environment and developing an appropriate course of action.

From our point of view, such theories provide a basic understanding of what motivates athletes to succeed, but, in practice, life is not so simple. What happens if the athlete finds that he has to give up too much in order to get what he wants? What about the athletes who won't maintain a consistent training programme because they prefer to have late nights out, to drink and smoke, to spend all available time studying for professional exams, or for whom the physical training demands are too great? Alternatively, what happens if the athlete gets what he wants and then rests on his laurels? He did it once, so everyone knows he could do it; he got the contract or the gold medal, so he doesn't need to do it again.

Sporting Bodymind has spent some time exploring this issue. We haven't come up with an all-embracing solution because every athlete has a different constellation of qualities and because motivating factors are almost always difficult to pin down. We have, however, had ample opportunity to work with the individuals who go beyond the normal demands made upon them, the athletes who are constant self-starters, with whom motivation is never an issue . . . and from such observations of what Abraham Maslow, the founding father of humanistic psychology, calls 'the Self Actualising Individual', a third model of motivation emerges.

This model is called the 'self actualising' 'or synergistic' factor. This lies *within* the athlete and, when his desire shifts from external gratification (whether through material goods or social approval), to meeting internal goals, he begins to become a self-starter.

Let's put it another way. An athlete, like any normal individual, needs certain things in order to be happy and fulfilled. We all need food, shelter, security, social recognition, love, acceptance, material comforts and entertainment. In the context of motivation, we take this idea a little further by presenting three major categories into which most of these needs fall. These categories are security, power and love. Let us consider each of them in turn.

- *Security* This is the starting point. An athlete needs to know that when he comes to a training session, he will have a place in the team and be playing in a position for which he feels qualified. He must believe that the coach won't be saying one thing to his face and another behind his back. If a professional, he will need a contract, a home and a steady source of income.

- *Power* The athlete needs to know that he is capable of doing the task at hand and that, within certain limits, his evaluation of the situation will receive support. A team player needs moments when he will have authority over other team mates. He may need fame and the ability to direct people's attention towards him. He will need money to obtain material goods and status to obtain what he can't get through money.

- *Love* An athlete needs love, though this isn't the word usually used. He needs recognition from spectators, from his friends and family. He needs approval from his coach. He needs admiration or respect from his fellow players. He needs acceptance of himself, his strengths and his weaknesses.

Now, as long as the athlete is trying to satisfy these needs *externally* from his environment, the ultimate sense of success will elude him – this is why you can find professionals who have tremendous financial contracts and still want more money, athletes who have worldwide recognition and still hunger for the spotlight on television. However, although desire for basic needs and avoidance of punishment *are* motivating factors, and all of us operate on this basis for greater or lesser periods of each day, there *is* a step further which the athlete can and sometimes does take.

When we talked about 'neurotic' versus 'creative' competitiveness, we were making a first approximation about motivation on the self-actualising level. As long as the athlete lacks the qualities of security, power and love and seeks them outside himself, he doesn't have control. His sense of *who he is* is dependent upon external things which he needs in order to feel that he is fulfilled by having them. The shift comes when the athlete begins to discover these qualities in *himself*. Instead of seeking approval, he finds his own sense of inner worth. Instead of needing to tell other people what to do, he has an inner sense of authority so that people listen to him when he speaks or seek out his advice. He becomes secure enough in himself to be able to take risks in his performance and know that he is still a valuable player when he fails. In other words, he becomes a self-motivator when he begins to discover that the qualities he was seeking in his environment are within *him* and can be expressed in his own play. He begins to embody the qualities in his performance, instead of seeking them outside himself.

Watching England goalkeeper, Ray Clemence, at team meetings it became obvious that he had no need to find security outside himself. Although he had a clear perspective on the team and the tactics of the game, he waited to be asked for his advice. He didn't need to demonstrate his knowledge. He didn't criticise other players. He was always prepared to take another look and accept responsibility for his own performance. Furthermore, of all the players in the team, he was the most generous with the secrets of his trade. Such qualities come from a security of belief in his own ability, skill and technique. He didn't need to flaunt his knowledge *and* he could take an honest look at himself without worrying what bogeys he would dig up. He was also passionate in his play and not afraid to show that he felt for the game.

Instead of seeking power, the self-motivator is given it. For example, Ossie Ardiles, the Argentine international and Tottenham team player, commanded a great deal of respect from his team mates. One player put it this way: 'When I'm playing with Ossie, I always know what he wants from me. I don't mean that I automatically do what he says. I mean that he is very clear without my being able to explain it. If he has the ball and is running with it, he may pass it to me. But I always know whether he wants me to take the ball and go with it, or if he is passing it to me to control whilst he moves into a position for me to pass it back. Sometimes, if I see a good opening, I'll run with it even if he wanted it back, but nine times out of ten I give it back, if he wants it. He's too great a player to quarrel with over who's going to control the field.' Though soft spoken and initially limited in English, Ossie commanded respect from his team mates because of his ability and his confidence in that ability.

Love takes the form of self-acceptance and self-recognition. We've often noticed that the athletes who seem most contented with themselves, their own company and their job, who like who they are and what they are doing, are very often the ones who are the cornerstone of team spirit and morale. They are the ones who exhort other athletes to do their best, who console those who are disappointed, who bounce back quickest from defeat

Volleyball – a synthesis of individual and team skills and an example of 'synergy' in action.

or difficulties. Their own self-esteem is not lacking and therefore they have no qualms about expressing their respect or care or admiration for others.

We are suggesting, then, that the athlete's shift from immaturity to maturity involves a shift from seeking to have his needs of security, love and power met by the outside, to finding these qualities in himself. He learns to express these qualities in his performance, in his relationship with his coach and team mates and throughout his life. It isn't surprising that athletes who are secure in their position and performance in their sport often have secure and stable family lives and established positions in the community in which they live. Their inner sense of security is drawn upon in areas of life other than that of their sport. Athletes who are generous with their time with their team mates also find time to give talks at youth clubs and charity events, and athletes who have an inner sense of power in their game often do equally well in their business life long after their sporting career is finished.

And so we come full circle back to competition and the difference between 'creative' and 'neurotic' competitiveness. The 'neurotic' competitor is one who wants to beat his opponent in order to measure up to some external standard. Such a competitor plays to gain something from the world outside, which he feels he needs or is lacking.

On the other hand, the 'creative' competitor uses sport to discover or draw out what he really is, in the faith that what he discovers will be good. He discovers and expresses his inner resources, his qualities and his motivation, as he competes, expanding the possibilities of ways for him to be. The more he discovers, the more he is moved to use sport as a means to find out who he is and what his purpose may be. How is he unique? What has he to offer the world?

Sport becomes a vehicle through which he is able to express himself... And instead of using it to achieve security, power and love, he now demonstrates to the world that he has these qualities inside himself already. This shift marks the beginning of the most impressive and satisfying stage of his sporting career.

Appendix A:
A twelve-week programme

Since forming *The Sporting Bodymind*, our work with a wide variety of sportspeople has led us to identify a number of common problems and to find techniques which seem best able to offer solutions. This information is compiled here in the form of a twelve-week programme of exercises which offers a basic introductory course on mental training.

It is possible to do all the exercises alone, although working under the supervision of your sports psychologist or coach would be somewhat easier. Each exercise is accompanied by its page reference. We suggest that you re-read some of the preceding text first, however, in order to understand better the specific object of the exercise. This will also help you to determine how the exercise can best help your sporting performance. The more successful you are in relating the exercises to your technical and tactical training, the easier and more enjoyable they will be.

The twelve-week format is divided into three sections. If you set aside a calendar month for each section you will have two or three days to review your progress before moving on. The exercises are divided into two streams, left- and right-brain techniques, each exercise developing or adding to the previous exercise of its type. Since the left-brain skills for any given week have been chosen to complement the right-brain skills of that same week, the two streams should be followed simultaneously. For example; in week three you should discover an affirmation whilst carrying out your *performance practice* which will reinforce that practice; the *likes and wishes* exercise of week eight can help you pin down the details of your *performance review*; in week ten the *visual re-editing* exercise is paired with a *goal-setting* exercise so you may work out a series of realistic targets to change an inappropriate attitude.

Although it is important to work at a regular rhythm (the ideal being the same period of time in the same place every day) you can spend more time on some exercises than others. However, it's better to complete the programme once and then go back to parts of it that need more work or which are particularly appropriate to your overall training than to get bogged down in one section for too long.

Weeks 1–4   Introductory techniques: Basic mental rehearsal

RIGHT BRAIN   LEFT BRAIN

Week 1

pages: | *pages:*

Relaxation and concentration   37–44

These two mental skills are the starting point for any visualisation – and are also invaluable in themselves. If you learn these techniques well, all of your subsequent visualisation exercises will be that much easier and more effective.

Warming-up checklist   11–20

Sit down and carefully make a warming-up checklist. Notice those categories in which you are competent and those which you ignore and forget. As the week progresses, add to the list as you begin to recognise other ways in which you warm-up.

Week 2

Black box   14–15
Right place/Right time   61

First, carry out a relaxation exercise, then perform the *black box* exercise. This should only take a few moments. Follow this immediately with the *right place/right time* exercise.

Evocative word   87
Warming-up checklist   11–20

Let an *evocative word* come to you in your *right place/right time* situation which captures the impact of this situation in your memory and write it down on a card. Continue to add to your checklist.

Week 3

Sitting relaxation   37–8
Performance practice   58–62

Learn a way to relax sitting up. This is the best way of preparing for a mental rehearsal.
The *performance practice* exercise is the first straightforward mental rehearsal. Choose a particular skill of importance in your sport which is not too difficult.

Affirmations   86–7

When you have carried out your *performance practice* for a few days find an *affirmation* which encapsulates the next goal you are working towards in that particular area of your sport. Write it down.

Week 4

Instant preplay   62–4
Instant replay   67–8

Now that you are beginning to learn how to visualise, use it in your training with *instant preplay* and *instant replay* exercises. It is best to focus on the same or similar skill to the one you have been using in your *performance practice*.

Meanwhile, continue to practise *performance practice* from week three at home.

Preview/review   77–86

Read the section on Preparation and Review and then do a *Preview/review* exercise after your next competition. At first you may want to make up your own exercise sheets similar to the one in the book to use after each performance for a while.

Weeks 5–8 Analysing your performance: More mental rehearsals

RIGHT BRAIN	LEFT BRAIN

Week 5

pages:

Ideal model   60
Choose a skill different from the one which was the subject of your *performance practice* and then do an *ideal model* exercise with it. Alternatively, you may want to focus on a more general quality of your performance rather than a specific skill or technique.

pages:

Deciding priorities   73–5
Now that you have had some time to evaluate how you prepare for your performance, and how you review that performance, you can take a look at your major sporting goals. Use the *deciding priorities* exercise to map out future goals, ambitions and strategies.

Week 6

'As if . . .' visualisation   64–7
Look back at the priorities you set last week in your left-brain exercise. Choose a particular quality you want to cultivate in your performance this week. Build an *'as if . . .'* visualisation round it.

'Wheel' of words   42–3
To help you cultivate the quality you have chosen for your *'as if . . .'* visualisation, build a *'wheel' of words* around that quality as well.

Week 7

Coloured liquid relaxation   38
Substitution rehearsal   61–2
Practise this alternative form of relaxation and see if you prefer it. Then carry out a *substitution rehearsal*; consider a part of your game which is giving you trouble and use this rehearsal to give a boost to your perspective in this area.

Preview/review check   77–86
Now that you have carried out the *preview/review* exercise a number of times, do one on your next competition and compare it with your very first one. How have you changed? Did you learn anything from one *preview/review* exercise to the next? What else do you need to do?

Week 8

Performance review   68–9
Now that you are thoroughly familiar with visualisation techniques, take the next opportunity to review a match with a *performance review*. During the rest of the week continue your mental rehearsal practice with any of the techniques you have already learned.

Likes and wishes   114–5
Complement your *performance review* with a *likes and wishes* exercise. Find out how to get the most out of each match or competition.

Weeks 9–12 Problem solving techniques

RIGHT BRAIN	LEFT BRAIN

Week 9

	pages:		pages:

Quiet place 94–6

It is now time to take a slightly more dispassionate view of your mental training and get away from it all! As you practise the *quiet place*, reflect under which conditions you would find this exercise most useful.

Evocative word no. 2 107–8
Deciding priorities 73–5

Choose an evocative word which captures the mood of your *quiet place* for you and make an *evocative word card* for it.

Take a look at your priorities of a month ago. How are you doing on your one-month priorities? What about your long-term priorities. Do you need to up-date your lists?

Week 10

Visual re-editing 98–9

Now that you have had a considerable experience using visualisation techniques and are more familiar with the types of problems you can solve with mental rehearsals, find a more complex or deep-seated problem whose solution needs something more than simple mental rehearsal. Use *visual re-editing* to create a change in your self-image.

Intermediate goal-setting 75–6

Set goals for ways in which you are going to deal with an attitudinal problem, an injury, or a particular area of your sport. Perhaps you can use the problem for which you are using the *visual re-editing* exercise. How are you going to organise yourself and your training to overcome this problem?

Week 11

'Transforming' your opponent 112–3

Having worked with an inner conflict, now explore a conflict you may have with a 'bogey' opponent.

Affirmation no. 2 86–7

Build an *affirmation* which reflects the new attitude you are developing towards your 'bogey' opponent. This will greatly reinforce your efforts to change the old attitude.

Week 12

'Wise person' exercise 130

When all else fails, this exercise can generate new ideas or approaches to old problems. Choose a problem which seems insoluble and apply this technique.

Preview/review of mental training course 77–86

Evaluate your performance on this twelve-week training course. How well did you do? Did you accomplish your goals? Which areas of your mental training need further work? What will you begin to work on next week? How will you maintain the benefits you have discovered?

Appendix B:
The Sporting Bodymind checklist

The following checklist identifies those areas where athletes most frequently find their mental skills and abilities challenged and shows where in the book you can find techniques which can help you to meet such challenges. Having turned to the relevant pages, read the introductory paragraphs to get a clear idea of the approach suggested and then choose the technique that appeals to you most.

FACTOR OR CHALLENGE	GENERAL TIPS		SPECIFIC EXERCISE	
		pages:		*pages:*
Aggression, development of			*'As if . . .' visualisation*	64–7
Anger, loss of temper	Warming-up Attitudes and change	12–13 101–16	*Simulating referee* *Black box*	12–13 14–15
Anxiety	Dealing with anxiety	89–99	*Black box* *'As if . . .'* *Affirmations* *visualisation* *Positive self- imagery* *Segmenting goals* *Changing fear into excitement* *Changing anxiety into energy* *Catastrophic expectations* *Creative distraction* *Quiet place* *Focusing on a movement pattern* *Building routine of task-oriented patterns* *Visualising music* *Progressive desensitisation* *Visual re-editing*	14–15 64–7 86–7 92 93 93 93 93–4 94 94–6 96 96–7 96 98 98–9

FACTOR OR CHALLENGE	GENERAL TIPS		SPECIFIC EXERCISE	
		pages:		*pages:*
Bad techniques	Body awareness	21–32	*Slowing down*	55
	Attitudes and		*mental rehearsal*	
	change	101–16	*Instant replay*	67–8
Body co-ordination, difficulties with			*Basic performance practice*	58–60
Confidence, loss of	Team spirit	117–137	*'As if . . .' visualisation*	64–7
Concentration, loss of	Relaxation and concentration	39–45	*Concentration exercises*	42–4
			Instant preplay	62–4
			Affirmations	86–7
Conflict with team mates	Warming-up	15–18	*Gestalt dialogue*	113–14
	Team spirit	117–137		
	Attitudes and change	101–16		
Conflict with coach	Attitudes and change	101–16		
Chattering mind	Body awareness	21–32	*Black box*	14–15
	Analytical thinking	88	*Key moments*	30
			Quiet place	94–6
Criticism, positive	Analytical thinking	71–88	*Encouraging honesty*	128–9
	Attitudes and change	101–16	*Appreciations*	131
	Team spirit	135–6	*Performance review*	68–9
Distractions	Warming-up	11–20	*Simulating distractions*	12–13
	Attitudes and change	101–16	*Black box*	14–15
			Quiet place	14–16
			Likes and wishes	114–15
			Energising the opposite	115–16
Defeatism, depression	Attitudes and change	101–16	*'As if . . .' visualisation*	64–7
	Team spirit	117–37	*Ideal model*	60

FACTOR OR CHALLENGE	GENERAL TIPS		SPECIFIC EXERCISE	
		pages:		*pages:*
			Affirmations	86–7
			Esalen word game	106–7
			Evocative word cards	107–8
			Exploring polarities	109
Defeat, making most of	Analytical thinking	71–88	*Performance review*	69–9
	Team spirit	117–37	*Preview/review*	77–86
Enthusiasm, loss of	Attitudes and change	101–16	*Ideal model*	60
			Affirmations	86–7
			Esalen word game	106–7
			Evocative word cards	107–8
			Exploring polarities	109
Environment, making friends with	Warming-up	12–14	*Like and wishes*	114–15
	Attitudes and change	114–16	*Energising the opposite*	115–16
Fear	Dealing with anxiety	89–99	*Affirmations*	86–7/92
			Changing fear into excitement	93
			Progressive desensitisation	98
			Visual re-editing	98–9
Form, loss of	Relaxation and concentration	33–45	*Body awareness exercises*	26–30
	Top performance and visualisation	60–1	*Performance practice*	58–62
			Substitution rehearsal	61–2
Gains, capitalising on	Team spirit	117–37	*Top performance visualisation*	60–1
			Instant preplay	62–4
			Instant replay	67–8
			Preview/review	77–86
Goal-setting	Warming-up	18	*Deciding priorities*	73–5
	Visualisation	52–3	*Intermediate goal-setting*	75–6
	Analytical thinking	73–6	*Segmenting goals*	93
	Team spirit	133–4	*Brain-storming*	129

FACTOR OR CHALLENGE	GENERAL TIPS		SPECIFIC EXERCISE	
		pages:		*pages:*
Hostile crowds	Warming-up	12–14	*Simulating distractions*	*12–13*
	Attitudes and change	114–16	*Likes and wishes*	*114–15*
Inconsistency	Body awareness	21–32	*Instant preplay*	*62–4*
	Relaxation and concentration	33–45	*Instant replay*	*67–8*
Indecision			*'As if . . .' visualisation*	*64–7*
Injury, recovery from	Analytical thinking	75–6	*Basic performance practice*	*58–60*
	Team spirit	123–134	*Affirmations*	*86–7*
			'As if . . .' visualisation	*64–7*
			Intermediate goal-setting	*75–6*
Jitters/nerves	Warming-up	11–20	*Black box*	*14–15*
	Dealing with anxiety	88–99	*Instant preplay*	*62–4*
			Positive self-imagery	*92*
			Segmenting goals	*93*
			Changing fear into excitement	*93*
			Changing anxiety into energy	*93*
			Catastrophic expectations	*93–4*
			Quiet place	*94–6*
			'As if . . .' visualisation	*64–7*
			Focusing on a movement pattern	*96*
			Building a routine of task-oriented patterns	*96–7*
Peak experience	Attitudes and change	101–16	*Top performance visualisation*	*60–1*
Psyched out, put off by opponent	Attitudes and change	109–14	*Ideal model*	*60*
			Changing anxiety into energy	*93*

FACTOR OR CHALLENGE	GENERAL TIPS		SPECIFIC EXERCISE	
		pages:		*pages:*
			I see . . . I imagine . . . and that makes me feel	111
			Analysis	112
			'Transforming' your opponent	112–13
Priorities, setting them	Analytical thinking	73–5	*Deciding priorities*	73–5
			Intermediate goal-setting	75–6
	Team spirit	119–31	*Preview/review*	77–86
			Discussion meetings	119–20
Qualities, cultivating them	Attitudes and change	101–16	*'As if . . .' visualisation*	64–7
			Affirmations	86–7
			Evocative word cards	107–8
			Slogans	87–8
			Esalen word game	106–7
			Exploring polarities	109
Relaxation	Relaxation and concentration	33–8	*Relaxation exercises*	37–8
	Visualisation	50		
Self-image, cultivating a positive	Visualisation	46–69	*'As If . . .' visualisation*	64–7
	Attitudes and change	106–9	*Ideal model*	60
			Affirmations	86–7
			Evocative word cards	107–8
			Slogans	87–8
			Esalen word game	106–7
			Exploring polarities	109
Strategies, developing them	Analytical thinking	71–86	*Deciding priorities*	73–5
			Preview/review	77–86
	Team spirit	117–137	*Brain-storming*	129

FACTOR OR CHALLENGE	GENERAL TIPS		SPECIFIC EXERCISE	
		pages:		*pages:*
Stamina			*'As if . . .' visualisation*	*64–7*
			Affirmations	*86–7*
			Evocative word cards	*107–8*
Solving problems	Attitudes and change	101–16	*Substitution rehearsal*	*61–62*
	Team spirit	117–37	*Stepping outside self*	*113–14*
			Brain-storming	*129*
			Imagining self as coach	*129*
			Wise person	*130*
Twitching	Attitudes and change	101–16	*Breathing*	*28–9*
			Exaggeration	*29*
			'As if . . .' visualisation	*64–7*
Team spirit	Warming-up	15–17	*Slogans*	*87–8*
	Team spirit	117–37	*Appreciations*	*131*
			Circle check	*127*
Tension	Relaxation and concentration	33–40	*Black box*	*14–15*
	Dealing with anxiety	89–99	*Kinaesthetic body inventory*	*26–7*
			Breathing	*28–9*
			Exaggeration	*29*
			Relaxation exercises	*37–8*
			Segmenting goals	*93*
			Changing fear into excitement	*93*
			Catastrophic expectations	*93–4*
			Creative distraction	*94*
			Quiet place	*94–6*
Team meetings	Warming-up	18		
	Team spirit	119–31		
Training	Body awareness	21–32	*Instant preplay*	*62–4*
	Visualisation	46–69	*Instant replay*	*67–8*
	Analytical thinking	71–86	*Slogans*	*87–8*
	Team spirit	133–35		

FACTOR OR CHALLENGE	GENERAL TIPS	pages:	SPECIFIC EXERCISE	pages:
Techniques (skills), maintaining	Body awareness	21–32	*Performance practice* *Right place/ right time*	58–62 61
Techniques (skills), changing	Body awareness Attitudes and change	21–32 101–16	*Eyes closed practice* *Colour coding body* *Breathing* *Changing handedness* *Exaggeration* *Instant preplay* *Instant replay*	26–8 28 28–9 29 29 62–4 67–8
Unrealistic goals	Analytical thinking Team spirit	73–6 133–4	*Deciding priorities* *Segmenting goals* *Discussion meetings*	73–5 93 119–20
Warming-up	Warming-up Analytical thinking	11–20 76–82	*Black box* *Preview/review* *Changing fear into excitement* *Changing anxiety into energy* *Creative distraction*	14–15 77–86 93 93 94

Appendix C: Alphabetic list of techniques and exercises